THE COYOTE HUNTER

A complete guide to
tactics, equipment and techniques
for hunting North America's perfect predator

By Don Laubach, Mark Henckel
and Merv Griswold

1 2 3 4 5 6 7 8 9 0 MG 05 04 03 02 01 00

Library of Congress Catalog Card Number 00-133335
ISBN 1-58592-043-6

Published by:
Don Laubach
Box 85
Gardiner, MT 59030

Publishing consultant:
SkyHouse Publishers, an imprint of Falcon® Publishing, Inc.,
Helena, Montana.

Illustrations by Jim Stevens.
Front and back cover photos by Jim Hamilton.

Printed in the United States of America.

TABLE OF CONTENTS

INTRODUCTION

THE COYOTE HUNTER

Just forty-five seconds of film. That's all it took.

We had been shooting film for a coyote-hunting video. And, frankly, it hadn't been going all that well.

First off, there were four of us. That's really two too many for ideal coyote hunting.

Also, there was the camera. That causes problems of its own. You have to get coyotes to come in at the right angle. You have to get the coyotes, the caller, and the shooters in the frame properly. You have to train your shooters when to shoot and when not to shoot to get it on the video.

That winter day, we had just finished calling in a pair of coyotes in another drainage. We had shot neither of them. Things just weren't right to get it on film. It had gone the same way with the other coyotes we called in that day.

As a result, there was more than a little frustration traveling in that vehicle as we headed to yet another spot to try calling again. We had done all the other things right that day. We had identified an area with a good coyote population. We had scouted the area well. We'd played the wind right. We'd made good setups. We had called in coyotes.

We were driving down a gravel road when we spotted two coyotes going up a nearby hill. That's not exactly the textbook way to locate game when you're coyote hunting. And I suppose we could have jumped out and tried shooting at them right there.

But we decided instead to drive down the road a ways. We'd try filming one more time. We'd hide the vehicle, walk about 250 yards, then set up in a little basin where the coyotes would likely be over the hill ahead of us.

The caller and the two shooters went down the hill to a little knoll and tried to get set up quickly while I positioned the camera up on the slope behind them. As it turned out, that gave me the best vantage point for that forty-five seconds of film.

My three partners, as it turned out, landed right in the middle of some cactus, with the caller lying down in spikes in the middle, while the two shooters impaled themselves on cactus spikes on both sides of him.

The caller then made the first rabbit-in-distress sounds with his hand call, just as I turned on the camera.

What those three partners couldn't see were those two coyotes—which appeared almost instantly at the head of that little basin.

As the caller made his next sound, the first coyote started running down the slope, then stopped amid the sagebrush, yellow grass, and patches of snow. My partners couldn't see the coyote.

When the caller made his next sound, the second coyote started running and ran past the first one, trying to get to that suffering rabbit first. Then they both started running, straight down the slope, straight toward the caller and two shooters. Nope, my partners couldn't see that either.

In fact, it wasn't until a few seconds later, when one of the shooters moved to try to get out of the cactus, that things really got interesting.

In less time than it takes to read this sentence, the film recorded the near collision. The coyotes spotted the caller and hunters. The caller and hunters spotted the coyotes.

At one point, the coyotes and hunters were separated by just three steps, and the coyotes were still running at full speed. It took just a moment more for the coytotes to kick their speed into an even higher gear and race past the hunters. They were just a blur as they disappeared over the hill.

Not a shot was fired. It all took just forty-five seconds of film. All that remained were my three partners, now bristling with cactus spikes.

As we shook our heads and laughed about it afterwards—and even now as I laugh about it again—it strikes me that the incident was, oh, so typical of coyote hunting.

If you know about coyotes, if you get into the right area, if you make the right sounds, and if you get set up just right, you not only can call in coyotes, you can have things happen all around you in an amazingly short—and unbelievably exciting—period of time.

There are plenty of areas with enough coyotes living in them to make these things happen. All it takes are some coyote-hunting skills.

As for filming videos, that's something we also do that sometimes gets in the way of being the most effective hunters we can be. We could shoot more. But filming sometimes gets in the way. And we still do shoot our share of coyotes.

On a combination coyote-hunting/filming trip last winter, for example, we wound up calling in thirty-one coyotes in three days. We shot nine of them. We passed on other shots we could have taken had we not been filming.

It's a bit more comfortable writing a book about coyote hunting. No camera angles to worry about. No cactus spikes. No big decisions on when to shoot and when not to shoot. And the only unnatural sound you make is when you mumble into the tape recorder, or hit a bad keystroke on the computer, then curse about it a bit.

Writing a book about coyote hunting does let you do other things as well. You can pause and remember all those things that go into becoming a successful coyote hunter. You can remember the smell of the sagebrush, the crispness of a winter morning, the excitement of spotting a coyote and then calling him in.

The purpose of this book is to help others experience and enjoy those same things—without the cactus spikes. It's to help the beginner get started. It's to open some new horizons for hunters well on their way. It's to tweak some memories among the veterans of coyote hunting and verify what they've seen and experienced on their own.

Since this is a three-author endeavor, you may be puzzled by the fact that the words "I" and "we" are used throughout the book, but the identities of the "I" and "we" aren't split apart. The reason is that the book simply reads better this way. It's an instructional book, and the important thing is that you understand what we're talking about, rather than who did this or who did that. Also, aside from the individual stories, the views here are pretty much agreed upon by all of us.

Far more important is the message about coyotes, coyote hunting, and coyote hunters. Coyotes are truly impressive and adaptable predators. Coyote hunters must learn and grow to effectively go after them. And coyote hunting is a challenge today and a look to the future as a tool to manage these animals so that all wildlife—and people, too—can co-exist in coyote country.

Don Laubach
Gardiner, Montana

Merv Griswold
Gillette, Wyoming

Mark Henckel
Park City, Montana

CHAPTER ONE

THE COYOTE

Picture the perfect predator. That perfection is the coyote. No other predatory mammal in North America is so adaptable and so widespread into different habitats. From Maine to Mexico and Alaska to Florida, coyotes have carved out their niche in the natural world around them. They survive—and thrive—in the hardwood forests of the East, the deserts of the Southwest, the deep snow country of the upper Midwest, the high peaks of the Rockies, the open farm country of the Great Plains, even the suburbs of major cities all across the continent.

Coyotes can live on mice and insects. They can pull down antelope or deer. Small game like rabbits, upland birds, prairie dogs, and squirrels are all food for the coyote. They'll kill sheep and calves, munch happily on carrion, and steal animals killed by other predators.

An old saying goes in the West that if the world were to end, the last sound on earth would be the howl of a coyote.

No other animal seems so durable, so persistent, so all-encompassing, so versatile, so tough.

Perhaps that's the reason why coyote hunting has become so popular in recent years. In the old days, it used to be fur prices or livestock damage control that pitted man against coyotes. Back then, it was nothing short of an all-out war. More recently, however, as much as anything, it's the challenge of matching wits with a perfect predator and helping agricultural interests effectively manage coyotes that has sparked new interest in coyote hunting.

To be a coyote hunter, however, you've got to know something about the animal you're hunting. The more you know, the more effective a hunter you can be. And I'm guessing that, in the process, you'll also come to appreciate this animal for all his natural perfection—the most perfect of predators.

Coyotes not only scratch out a living, but thrive, in a variety of environments and feed on a variety of food sources. This coyote is catching mice.
Jim Hamilton photo.

The Basics

Coyotes are a member of the dog family. Their Latin name is *Canis latrans,* which, literally translated, means "barking dog." They're relatives of the wolf, the fox, and our own domestic dogs.

Size in coyotes can vary widely, depending on where you find them. Adults can weigh as little as twenty pounds or as much as fifty. Desert coyotes of the Southwest are usually smaller. Northern coyotes are more toward the larger end of the spectrum. In our area of Montana and Wyoming, the average male weighs about thirty pounds. They're about four feet in length from the tip of their nose to the tip of their tail. They're about fifteen to twenty inches high at the shoulder.

When you talk about how a coyote looks, there are some things that are the same among all coyotes, while other attributes vary. All coyotes have the distinctive upright ears, the narrow muzzle, and the round, bushy tail. But the color of coyotes ranges widely and is one of the many ways that these animals are so well adapted to the world in which they live.

Coloration in coyotes can vary quite a bit, depending on where you find them. If anything, it's like a natural camouflage, suited perfectly to where they live.

In open country, coyotes will have more splotchy grays and whites. In timber country, there will be more red on them and more dark gray. Everywhere, coyotes seem to have developed coloration that helps them blend into the world around them.

The key to all things for a coyote is food. An adult coyote needs to eat two to three pounds of food per day. Big litters require a lot of food. And prey must be abundant for young, inexperienced coyotes to be able to catch enough to fill their bellies. Ample food means ample coyotes. Lean times mean fewer coyotes. However, whatever the conditions, coyotes have been blessed with natural tools that help them hunt for food.

These predators are athletes built to cover ground easily. They can walk at a pace of about four miles per hour. At a trot, they can cover about eight miles per hour. At a dead run, they've been clocked at more than forty miles per

Coyotes can vary a great deal in size and coloration, with northern coyotes generally larger than southern coyotes. This Wyoming coyote is a good-sized one. Jim Hamilton photo.

hour. And, you have to remember, all this is over rough, broken terrain. It's not on a track field. Suffice it to say, they move along easily and can be extremely fast when they need to be.

Coyotes have extremely keen senses to help them in their hunting. Their sense of hearing is extremely sharp, and they can pick up even low noises at great distances. Their sense of smell is also highly developed, both to detect danger and to locate food. While their eyesight comes in third as a defense and food-gathering mechanism, it can't be ignored. Their eyes can pick up movements at considerable distances, and they can pick out a shape that doesn't belong in the world around them.

Coyote density in an area is directly related to the food supply. The more food there is available, the more coyotes the area can support and the smaller the size of each coyote's territory. In areas with little food, territories must be larger and coyote numbers are smaller.

Female coyotes are especially tied to a particular territory, while male coyotes may straddle the territories of several females. Territories can change by the season, as well. In summer, when food is abundant, a coyote's territory can be smaller. In winter, when food is scarce, territorial boundaries may crumble as coyotes are forced to hunt over larger areas.

Family Life

You might say that the coyote year begins in January since the first breeding pairs begin to get together then. Mating generally takes place between January and March. Pups are born about two months later.

The pups will be born in dens that coyotes dig out. Dens are often on south-facing slopes, reflecting the weather in April and early May when most pups are born. At that time of year, south-facing slopes benefit from the heat of the sun, making them warmer for pups who happen to be out early in the day.

Often, denning areas will have several holes. There's the hole that is occupied by the coyotes. The other holes are often called clean-out holes. These are places where, when the original den gets cluttered or the coyotes get bumped or disturbed, the pups can be moved.

Another characteristic of denning can be an exit hole, providing an alternate means of escape for the coyotes. If the den is on a ridge, these exit holes are often on the other side from the main entrance.

Coyotes often dig their dens relatively close to a water source. In the first weeks of life, the pups will rely on their mother's milk for nutrition. But by the time they're about three weeks old, they'll be on a semi-solid diet. From that time on, reliable water will become increasingly important in their lives.

For that reason, look for dens within a quarter mile, or half mile, of a permanent water source. It has been my experience that natural water sources are better than man-made ones. Springs, seeps, or ponds are preferred over stock tanks. But whatever the source, make sure it's permanent. Their instinct tells them that it has to be a water source that never fails.

Coyote den sites are most often relatively close to available water sources. If you're looking for coyotes in spring, look for water sources first. Jim Hamilton photo.

After about two weeks, the pups open their eyes. They emerge from the den for the first time a few days later. But in those first weeks of life, they stay close to the den. Both parents will bring food back to them.

At an age of five to seven weeks, they begin moving around more with their parents, learning the basics of hunting. How long the family group stays together—and how many of the pups survive—will usually be determined by food supply.

Pups can stay with the family unit up to about a year, finally being forced out when the next breeding season begins. But lone young coyotes will often strike out much earlier than that, as soon as their hunting skills allow them to kill enough to survive on their own.

Hunting is often done at night, and it's often in late spring and early summer when coyotes can get into trouble with ranchers. They end up killing just for fun and not eating what they kill, just learning the technique.

Coyotes can have a long life span. In the wild, they can live twelve to fifteen years. One coyote was recorded that lived more than eighteen years. But the attrition rate can be high in the coyote world.

While some litters of pups have numbered as high as fifteen to seventeen, the average litter size is six to eight pups.

But no matter how big or small the litter, many never reach maturity. Mortality is high for the pups. Making the transition from young coyote to adulthood can be hazardous as well, with many failing to reach breeding age.

Coyote Communication

When you talk about coyote communication, remember that you're treading on some awfully shaky ground. Every coyote hunter knows what he or she hears. But experienced hunters also know that every coyote sounds just a little different, just as different people talk differently. Some people talk a lot. Others say few words. Some say things one way. Others say things another.

If you want to keep it simple, coyotes make sounds that are sometimes called "bark-howls" or "yip-howls." They'll do barking or yipping and follow it with a long howl. That's pretty much what most of us hear. That's how you know a coyote is in an area.

Once you get past that, you begin to guess what the coyotes are doing and why they're doing it. Some people have broken it down into different types of howls—domain calls, or female invitation calls, or sunrise serenades. They talk about long howls, short howls, and aggressive howls.

What do these howls all mean? It would be so easy to know that if you heard a coyote making a certain sound, then the coyote trotted up to you and said, "I'm trying to call in a female." Or it said, "I'm being aggressive right now." Or the coyote said, "Don't mind me. I'm just serenading the sunrise." But until a coyote does that, we don't really know what they're saying.

That's not to say there aren't some insights we can make into coyote communications. And there's some fun in the guesswork, too, imagining what the coyotes are really saying.

In the evening, for example, when coyotes get ready to begin hunting, they tend to howl. Other coyotes will answer. There's no doubt in my mind that they're communicating with one another, saying something like, "I'm over here. I'm going to begin my hunting." Other groups will answer back, "We're here. We're going to be hunting in this area." To me, this evening howling has always been coyote groups establishing their whereabouts, letting others know where they are.

In the early morning, when a night's hunting is done, coyotes will often sing out the same way. It's usually not as long and not as vigorous, but it's as if they're telling other coyotes in the area that the hunt is over. They're going to lay up for the day on this ridge or in that draw. And where are the other coyotes going to spend the day?

I'm convinced that coyote howling in the middle of the night is also individuals or groups of coyotes communicating with each other. Lone coyotes, or young coyotes, might be looking for some companionship. It might be a locator just to make sure which other coyotes might be in the area.

Coyotes can make a wide variety of sounds, and some coyotes are more vocal than others. But we're really just guessing as to what coyotes are saying to each other. Jim Hamilton photo.

Chapter One ■

I'm also convinced that, when there's a kill, coyotes will communicate with other coyotes. Once a coyote has made a kill, every other coyote in the area will know about it. They'll come in and help clean it up. The dominant coyotes that made the kill will eat first. But if it's a big animal, others will get their chance to feed as well.

That wouldn't take place if it was simply a rabbit that a coyote caught and killed. But ranchers have told stories of how, in one night, a big calf will be completely cleaned up by coyotes. All around it, the ground is packed with coyote tracks. There simply must be a way that coyotes invite each other to join in a feed like that.

It should also be noted that coyote pups are very vocal— about like human kids. In the spring of the year, when the pups first start venturing outside the den, they'll often start yapping and barking while their parents are away hunting. That's one way you can locate dens early in the morning. When that takes place, the parents often come back to quiet the pups. And like human children, when the parents return and lay down the law, it gets quiet in the vicinity of the den very quickly.

Coyote Food

Coyotes are what are called opportunistic predators. They'll do whatever it takes to fill their bellies. They'll also make the most of whatever is most abundant and easiest for them to catch and eat.

In talking about what coyotes eat, it might be easier to say what a coyote doesn't eat. A coyote doesn't eat trees—and even saying that, they probably do chew on bark occasionally. They can and do eat insects, including grasshoppers. They thrive in the big mouse years or when ground squirrels are abundant. They love to hunt prairie dog towns. Cottontail and jackrabbits are perfect food items. They'll hunt ground-nesting birds and eat the eggs and the birds, if they can catch them. Coyotes will eat fruit and berries. I've seen hillsides where they've dug up roots to feed on.

Coyotes are opportunistic feeders, taking what's easiest and most available. As ranchers can tell you, that includes domestic livestock, especially sheep.

In suburban areas, they'll feed on dog food, pick through garbage, and feast on a poodle or a house cat with great relish. In agricultural areas, they can be amazingly bold at calving and lambing time, moving close to houses and ranch yards to kill calves and lambs.

During the fawning time of May, I've watched them sit on hillsides above the sagebrush flats where antelope does drop their fawns. The coyotes will watch the does drop the fawns, then move in quickly for an easy meal of antelope fawn. They'll take mule deer and whitetail fawns when they can find them. They can take down an elk calf easily within its first days of life and do the same with a newborn moose or bighorn sheep.

Anything that looks even close to edible will be a meal for a coyote. And that includes the leftovers from other predators like wolves, mountain lions, bears, and eagles. Coyotes draw from a variety of hunting techniques. They also have the ability to adjust their tactics when situations change.

A lone coyote or a pair of coyotes can get along nicely when the most available prey is rabbit size. If small-game populations drop and coyotes get in a situation where antelope or deer are the most available prey, they'll form packs.

Available food can also determine the social behaviors of coyotes. This is another measure of the adaptability of this predator. When mouse or rabbit numbers are high, more lone coyotes and coyote pairs will be apparent. During low population cycles for these smaller prey animals, coyotes may have to switch to bigger game like antelope or deer and will form packs to better hunt these big-game species.

Coyotes will also learn specific techniques to make their hunting easier. I can remember talking to wildlife biologists who were studying mule deer in the rough country bordering the Missouri River and Fort Peck Reservoir in Montana. They talked about coyotes that would literally set up relays to run deer to exhaustion. One coyote would chase the deer in a big circle, and when the deer came around, another coyote would begin the chase while the first one rested. Eventually, the deer would play out, and the coyotes could move in for the kill.

In addition to catching their own food, coyotes will also feed on carrion or the leftovers of kills by other predators. Jim Hamilton photo.

Another favored technique was to chase the deer out of the rough hills and onto the slick winter ice of the reservoir. On the ice, the coyotes had much better footing than the deer did. And when the deer finally slipped, the coyotes would move in for the kill.

Faced with a poor rabbit population, the coyotes quickly adjusted to new and bigger prey and were able to survive by taking down mule deer that were much bigger than they were.

In short, coyotes are opportunists. They'll take the easiest thing to catch. And older coyotes will teach younger coyotes just how it's done. And when it's necessary, they'll adapt to survive.

Survivors

Never underestimate the coyote's ability to survive. That's true of individual coyotes. It's true of coyotes as a species.

Coyotes have survived all the poisons and the trapping and the all-out war that was waged on them across the West for decades. Still, man has not been able to eradicate them from any areas. In recent times, in fact, coyote country has grown. It now spreads from the Atlantic to the Pacific and from the far North deep into Central America.

Predator-prey balance means taking some out of the population every year. But even when a disease like mange cuts deeply into a local population, coyote numbers seem able to bounce back quickly within a few years.

As to the toughness of individual coyotes, I'm reminded of individual animals that I've watched or taken.

One was a three-legged coyote that lived in the area around my house. The right front leg of that coyote was completely gone, right at the shoulder. Whether a wolf got it or the animal was attacked by another coyote, whether it was trapped or its leg was lost in a car collision, I don't really know.

During the summer, when I'd see that coyote and its hair was short, I could see where the tip of the bone was sticking out of the shoulder about two inches, covered over with skin or callous or something. In winter, long hair would cover the spot.

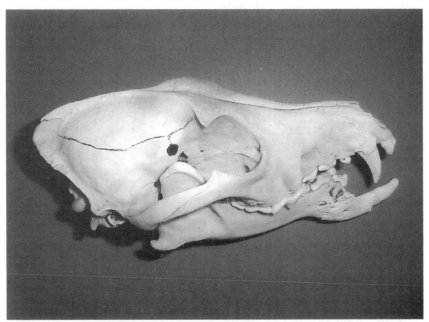

The jaw of this coyote shows it had been broken in some mishap long ago, but had healed well enough so that the animal was big and healthy when it was taken by a hunter.

This three-legged coyote traveled through our country for quite a while. One day, I was watching that coyote and another four-legged coyote hunt rock chucks—marmots—together. The three-legged coyote was the decoy. It kept the attention of the chucks. The four-legged coyote would then sneak in and make the kill. They were hunting as a team. And when the kill was made, the four-legged coyote ran off and the three-legged coyote joined him. They fed on the rock chuck together.

It was a great case of coyotes making the most of a situation. It ended with both coyotes getting a meal.

Another coyote I remember was one that I called in and killed. When skinning the coyote, I noticed that its lower jaw had been injured. In fact, the lower jaw had been broken completely in two. One lower canine tooth was missing. The upper tooth was broken off. This coyote had probably been kicked in the mouth by a domestic animal or a deer.

By the time I got him, the jaw had healed completely. The broken bones were fused together. And the coyote showed no signs of suffering from the disability. He was extremely fat and healthy. He had healed up and survived.

These individual coyotes are not alone in my experience, either. Over the years, there have been a number of coyotes with deformed legs, broken bones that have healed, disabilities that they've survived.

Each of them looked healthy. Each of them had overcome its injuries. Each one had survived. Say what you want about them, you've got to agree that coyotes are a tough breed. They're survivors. And they're perfect predators, able to scratch out a living wherever they're found and able to thrive and expand their range—in a day and age when many other predators are simply holding their own.

CHAPTER TWO

BASIC EQUIPMENT

Coyote hunting doesn't have to be a big-dollar pastime. You can get by with the most basic equipment. If you choose, on the other hand, you can spend more.

In coyote hunting, it's all a matter of what you've got and what you choose to invest in the pastime.

Maybe all you've got is gas money. Maybe you've got a hundred bucks to spend. Maybe you've got a thousand. Maybe money is no object at all.

In truth, the bottom line for all coyote hunters—no matter what their means—is to spend whatever money they want on the sport, but to spend their money wisely.

Put in its simplest terms, that means you can own camouflage for all occasions, or separate suits for different coyote environments. You can cozy up to a single rifle and use it for years. Or maybe you want to own several. In fact, all your equipment can be dealt with this way.

We're not here to tell you what you need to spend. We'll

just give you some hints on how to spend that money on basic equipment. We'll tell you what works. We'll tell you what to avoid. The rest—including coming up with the money for it—is up to you.

Camo and Clothing

To make the most out of your camouflage choices and your clothing purchases, you've got to understand the reason you're wearing camouflage clothing in the first place. And in the process, you should understand that there was a time in the coyote-hunting past when camouflage didn't even exist as we know it today.

Even though camo clothing is a big part of the industry now, with matching pants, shirts, coats, caps, even boots—it wasn't that critical in years past to have all those matching items. Even today, in a lot of the hunting we do in our part of the West, we basically wear overalls, maybe a camo jacket over the top, and some type of hat.

Mixing various types of camouflage will actually hide you better than wearing all one pattern. In this photo, the hunter is wearing three types and also has his rifle camouflaged.

That being said, let's talk first about fabrics. As important as the pattern of clothing you buy is the fact that your clothing must be soft, warm, and comfortable. You don't want hard nylon scratching or clicking against itself. You want whatever movements you have to make to be quiet ones. You also want clothing that protects you from the wind and that will provide some warmth. Wind can really bite into you, especially in open country. Warm clothes are comfortable clothes. You'll be sitting for long periods of time, and if you're cold and miserable, you won't last long. On days that promise to be cold in the morning and warm up considerably during the day, consider layers of clothing. That way you can bundle up in the morning and shed clothes as the day wears on. Toward evening, when the temperature starts dropping, you can put some layers back on.

The next step in your clothing purchases is to think about why you buy camouflage. You do it to hide yourself—sometimes hiding yourself out in the open. You want to break up your outline. You want to blend into your surroundings.

For my part, I really don't like the matching sets of caps, tops, and pants. I like a pattern breakup. I may wear one type of pants, another camo pattern of coat, possibly even a third for the cap. Another thing you should realize is that the actual patterns in the camo really aren't that important and, for the most part, weren't designed with you in mind.

Most camouflage out on the market today is designed for eastern forests—so I guess if you're calling in coyotes in the East, you've got it made. But even then, the patterns tend to be so small in detail that they blend into a single color if you step back a hundred or so yards and look at them.

For this reason, the overall color of the camouflage is most important to me. In general, that means tan colors are best in the fall. Green colors are best in spring. In the open West, lighter colors are better than darker ones. In a snowy winter, you can't beat a good set of whites.

To get an idea of what you need, you really should do a little field testing. Just take your camo jacket and set it out on the hillside and step off a distance of about two hundred yards. Then turn around and look back at it. If your camo sticks out like a sore thumb, it's the wrong kind of camo.

Another thing to consider is that you're going to have to make some compromises. Coyote country is highly variable. Camo and colors that work well in one type of habitat aren't going to work as well in another type of habitat. Short of buying suits for all occasions, it's all a matter of figuring out what works best for most of your hunting.

You might not believe it, but that's even true of winter whites. I can remember buying a new set of whites for a hunt I was planning in Wyoming. There was snow on the ground everywhere, so it seemed like a good idea. But when I got out there, the white in that new suit of whites was so white that it almost looked like a glowing blue color. I put some dirt on the suit to break up the new blue, and later went back to my old paint-spattered white painter pants that had a little more age to them and hence were a bit yellower and a better match with the snow.

In much of the rest of my non-snow situations, I like to use a pair of light-colored Carhartt coveralls and hooded sweatshirts. If you're going to get serious about coyote hunting in our country, I wholeheartedly recommend those hooded sweatshirts. They cut the wind and keep your head and neck warm. And between those coveralls and the sweatshirts, they tend to wear like iron and give you plenty of years of service.

It almost goes without saying that any kind of camouflage you purchase won't help you a bit if you silhouette yourself against the skyline. Your camo should blend into the background—and you've got to put yourself in a position where you have a background.

Another hint about camo that helped me out when I was a novice coyote hunter—and that continues to help me today—is using netting or sheets. Before winter whites became a customized piece of clothing, a lot of us just took along old white bed sheets when we hunted coyotes in the snow. We just wrapped the sheets around us.

Coyotes have keen eyesight, and probably the best camouflage that a hunter can use is to sit absolutely still when he's out after coyotes. Jim Hamilton photo.

The sheets did more than just match the background when we were sitting. When we walked or moved, the sheets masked our leg movements. How critical is that? I can tell you that for elk hunting in rifle season, we thought we had a pretty good idea and made some gaiters out of fluorescent orange material. When our partner started walking on a distant slope, and those gaiters started moving back and forth, we could spot our partner a mile away. I'm sure a coyote could have spotted those flashing gaiters at a distance of a couple of miles.

In recent years, when I am out filming coyotes and coyote hunters, I like to take a sheet of camouflage netting with me. I use it to cover the camera and tripod when I sit behind it. It's almost like mosquito netting in a very light color. You can see through it. It's light and easy to carry. But it breaks up the outline of the person behind it, especially against that solid background.

Why are we even worrying about camo, and why are we so particular about it blending into the landscape where you plan to hunt? The biggest reason is that it will allow you to make a little movement. If you don't have it, the coyotes

Hunters should wear whites against a snowy background. One effective camouflage is simply a white bed sheet that you can wrap around yourself.

will pick up on your movements much more quickly.

Think about it. You're calling. A coyote hears you call. The coyote pinpoints where the call is coming from. It comes in looking for something in that spot. If it looks directly toward where the sound is coming from and sees you, it'll never come in close enough.

Rifles

Ready. Set. Let the arguments begin!

When it comes to coyote calibers, there are no shortages of opinions as to what the best rifle might be. Frankly, as for me, I'm not going to participate.

That doesn't mean there aren't some things you should look for in a coyote rifle. It also doesn't mean we don't have some pet rifles of our own.

What's most important is to have a good, solid flat-shooter. Coyote country is often big country. As a result, you may have to reach out with your rifle to touch a coyote.

Some of the good varmint calibers available are the .22-250, .25-06, .220 Swift, .243, and 6mm. All of these will shoot flat at 250 to 300 yards. Also, you want that rifle to be able to hold a tight group at that distance. To do that, you need to practice. You need to check the loads you're using in that rifle. You need to optimize the performance of both you and your weapon of choice.

A coyote is fairly small, and the kill zone is even smaller—roughly a five-inch circle. To consistently hit that spot and make humane kills, it's going to take a little work at the shooting bench and with your cross sticks. If you're shooting dead-on at 250 yards, you need to know where the bullet is hitting at 50 or 100 yards as well. If the coyote is out at 300 yards, you'll need to know the amount of bullet drop for that shot, too.

Once again, it all comes down to practice, remembering where the bullet hits and where you need to hold. For whatever the reason, it has been my experience that more coyotes are missed at close range than at 100 to 200 yards. Maybe hunters figure that close shot is too easy. They don't take the time to place the bullet well. They don't know how their rifle will shoot at close ranges. Take the time to practice at all distances. You'll get every possible shooting opportunity in coyote hunting.

That brings us to the topic of owning several coyote rifles versus owning just one. Do more rifles—one for each shooting situation or type of terrain—make you a better coyote hunter? Not necessarily.

I can remember hunting with several friends who had different calibers that they shot with. They'd go hunting and miss, or at least not hit with the regularity that they should have. They'd each say the rifle must be off the mark. They'd take another rifle out the next time, and the same thing would happen.

Many coyote hunters with multiple rifles will tape a shot chart to the stock of each of their rifles with the amount of bullet drop at various distances. That's good. But the problem with it is that you don't always get a chance to check that chart when there's a coyote coming in. Or if you do, the coyote spots your movement and it spoils the situation. Perhaps the strongest argument for the one-rifle coyote hunter is that he can remember how his rifle handles without looking at a chart. Maybe that's why so many of those one-rifle coyote hunters seem to be so deadly when it comes to the shooting end of the sport.

If they practice with that one rifle, it almost becomes a part of them. Some western hunters go so far as to use the same rifle for coyotes, antelope, deer, and varmints. If they do have a second rifle, it's the one that they save for elk hunting. And some hunters will use the same rifle for elk hunting, too, if it's a big enough caliber.

That brings us to the problem of what scope to put on your rifle. Probably the most common scope used today is a variable, with a range of magnification power. Most are three-to-nine power. Some are three-to-ten. If there's a problem with that, it's that hunters are attuned to shooting at long ranges and have the scope dialed up as far as it'll go. If a coyote presents itself at close range, the hunter looks through the scope and can only see hair. Dialing it down to a lower power takes some movement and time.

For that reason, there's a solid argument to be made for a fixed-power scope. A good quality four-power or six-power will service you well. Fixed-power scopes are also often a bit less expensive than the variables. That might make a better-quality scope more affordable. In the end, perhaps, budgeting the same money and getting better glass—so that the scope is crisp and clear—makes another good argument for a fixed-power scope.

Using the same power scope also works in other ways for you. If you're familiar with a four-power or six-power scope, you can often use it to judge the range of a coyote. A coyote at a certain distance looks a certain way. It fills a certain part of the rifle scope. With a variable scope, if you use it at different powers, you never get a chance to use it as a range aid.

The most important thing about your coyote rifle is not the caliber you're using. Instead, it's how well you can handle it at various ranges and how quickly and easily you can shoot a coyote with it when you have the opportunity. Jim Hamilton photo.

Chapter Two ■

As you can see, without starting an argument as to the perfect coyote rifle, our tendencies are to make the rifle as simple as possible and then to practice with it—a lot—so that you become most familiar with it. Why? The truth of the matter, based on our experience, is that things can happen very quickly in coyote country. In shooting the video *Bustin' Coyotes,* we went through a lot of different setups and called in a lot of coyotes. Often, the whole process—from the first call we made to shooting the coyote—took no more than two minutes. It can happen that fast. There isn't time to make calculations. There isn't time to adjust equipment. The simpler you make it on yourself, and the more streamlined you can make the thought process that goes into the shooting, the better off you are.

Shooting Sticks

When bipods first came on the market some years ago, we thought they were the answer to everything. You could attach them to your rifle. They swung up out of the way. Then, when you needed to make a steady shot, you could swing them down and you'd have a solid rest to shoot from.

It didn't take too many trips into the field, however, to realize that bipods had their limitations. While they were good for helping you zero in on a prairie dog standing on his mound—and the prairie dog would sit there for a long time in one spot—they weren't so handy for game that was more mobile.

In a coyote-hunting situation, you'd adjust the length of the legs of the bipod, get them settled in so that the rifle was square up and down, and then the coyote would move. In moving the rifle to a new target location, all of a sudden the rifle wasn't square up and down anymore. You'd have to either readjust the length of the bipod legs—or shoot off of one leg while the other waved around in the breeze.

In recent years, bipod manufacturers have solved that problem. They've made an adjustable saddle on the bipod

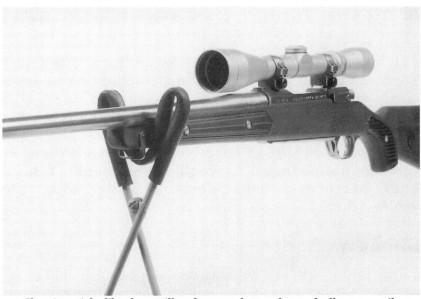

Shooting sticks like these will make you a better shot and offer a versatile rest in many shooting positions and in a variety of terrain.

that allows you to twist the rifle to the right or left to get it square. There's a bit of adjustment to help out the shooter with game that tends to move.

For my part, however, in between the time they came out with the first bipods and the time they came out with the new, improved models, I rediscovered shooting sticks, or cross-sticks. As a shooting aid, they have been used in the West since the days of the buffalo hunters. And everything that made them great as a shooting aid back then still serves shooters well today.

With shooting sticks, you have more freedom of movement. You can move with the coyote. Your crosshairs are still square—straight up and down. Shooting sticks also allow the shooter some freedom. By tipping them forward or back, you can use them prone or sitting. You can use them on hillsides. They're a lot faster.

Finally, make sure that the length of your bipods or shooting sticks are right for the type of shooting you expect to do. They come in various sizes for prone shooting, kneeling, or on hillsides.

Chapter Two ■

Should you buy shooting sticks or the new bipods? That's up to you. The bottom line is that either one will make you a better shooter because you can get a steadier hold. It's just a matter of which one best suits your needs.

One thing I'm sure of—once you start using a bipod or good, solid shooting sticks, you'll feel lost without them. They make you a better shot—no matter what rifle you're using.

Shoes or Boots

I'll admit it. I'm still looking for the perfect footwear for coyote hunting. I don't know if anyone is producing it or not. But I do know what I'm looking for.

The perfect footwear would come above the ankles to provide ankle support in the rugged country where coyote hunters sometimes wander.

The perfect footwear would be waterproof.

The perfect footwear would be comfortable in the cold and in the heat.

The perfect footwear would stop cactus from poking through and hurting your feet.

And, finally, the perfect footwear would have a tread that's rough enough to provide traction, but still shed mud.

As I said, I'm still looking for this item. Most of the footwear on the market fulfills some of these conditions, but falls down in others.

Hard Vibram soles, for example, provide good traction in warm conditions, but if Vibram gets cold, these soles can become exceedingly slick and turn into something akin to skis on a steep slope.

Leather boots are better than rubber in warm weather conditions, but rain, snow, or even a heavy morning dew can give you wet feet.

Rubber boots are waterproof, but they can be very hot to wear in warm weather conditions. And full rubber boots will hold in moisture from perspiration.

A coyote's nose is so sensitive that he can even detect the footprints that you leave behind, even if you're wearing rubber boots. Jim Hamilton photo.

My current choice is air bob soles. They're made of softer rubber and have little dimples that provide good traction. And you can walk quietly in them and have good gripping power on steep slopes. But in muddy conditions, they can pack with mud and it can be extremely difficult to shake that mud off.

Then, there's the matter of human scent.

A person would think that full rubber boots, or rubber-bottomed pacs would help keep human scent out of your tracks as you walk to and from your hunting area. While rubber bottoms might help, they aren't the total answer.

I can remember one time when I walked into a calling spot that overlooked a big basin. That's the area where I figured the coyote would be. Instead, when I started calling, it turned out the coyote was behind me.

As I watched that coyote coming in, he approached the trail where I had walked. As soon as he hit that trail, the calling setup was done. He left in a hurry in the opposite direction.

Another time, I was wearing full rubber boots—insulated—in a situation where I was calling in coyotes in the snow. This time, I had to walk to my calling location right up the bottom of a draw. I climbed the slope and sat down, sure that any coyotes that might come in would come across from other basins and be at about the same elevation as I was.

Instead, a coyote came in and dropped down into the bottom. When he got to my tracks in the snow, he stopped, sniffed, and then jumped over them. He wouldn't walk in my tracks. I was left wondering how he could smell my scent in the snow when I had those rubber boots on. But he got some kind of a scent that there was a human in the area and he never came in.

So, in thinking about it, add scent-free to my list of conditions for coyote-hunting boots. If the boots had that going for them—in addition to all the other qualifications—they'd be absolutely perfect.

Optics

One of the most critical things you need for coyote hunting in the West is an exceptionally good pair of binoculars. Without binoculars, it's about like hunting blind.

One thing that coyotes have that we don't have is that multiple coloration that blends them into any landscape out here. If a coyote isn't moving, he's very hard to see. That's why binoculars are such a plus.

The very minimum I'd have for magnification is 8-power. My favorite binoculars are 10-by-40 or 10-by-42. These are 10-power, with the second number identifying the field.

If they don't have binoculars, hunters are often forced to use their rifle scopes to look at distant objects. To do that, they've got to pick their rifles up. Then they put them down. Once again, it's unnecessary movement that can catch the eye of any coyote that might be coming in to their call.

Binoculars can help tell you whether a rock that looks like a coyote, or a bush that might be a coyote, really is a coyote.

Optics for a coyote hunter should include a good pair of binoculars for spotting and a rifle scope that can be operated simply and quickly. In fact, don't rule out the old straight 4-power scope.

If there's a disadvantage to looking through binoculars, it's that you only see a small portion of the landscape around you. If a coyote comes in from a different angle, you won't see it. So, even though you have a good pair of binoculars, don't look through them all the time. Use them intermittently, scanning the country, then put them down and use your eyes, then scan again.

Binoculars can also help you read animals. If you're calling to a coyote and he's still a distance away, you can read his reactions to the sound you're making. That can determine whether the sounds you're making are effective. It can also let you know when to call and when not to call.

Binoculars can also help you look for other animals that may tip you off that a coyote is coming in. In our part of coyote country, for example, magpies are often associated with coyotes. They'll follow them around in hopes of picking up an easy meal of leftovers. Many times, with my binoculars, I've spotted magpies that tipped me off that an unseen coyote was coming in.

Another fact of life in many parts of coyote country is that there are quite a few roads. Some might be gravel county roads. Others might be just two-rut tracks out across the prairie or off through the sagebrush.

When you travel these roads, a valuable tool to bring along is a good spotting scope. From these roads, especially in the morning when you use sirens, you can pick out coyotes at a distance that you can't see with binoculars. A spotting scope can pick out a coyote at a distance of a mile or more. By picking that animal out, you can decide where you're going to make your stands to call him in. You can also decide what route you might need to take to get into position.

You don't necessarily need to take the spotting scope along with you out into the field. Often, scopes are too bulky for that. But they are handy to keep in your vehicles and use when you need them.

Calls and Sirens

The sirens we use are optional. You don't really need one to hunt coyotes. But they can be a valuable tool for the coyote hunter.

There are several kinds of sirens that you can mount in your vehicle. In the old days, that was pretty much the only kind that was available. You'd get an old police siren and wire it up to your vehicle.

Today, many coyote hunters use portable sirens. They're a lot lighter. They don't require permanent installation. But they, too, are very handy to have.

The best time for using sirens is early in the morning, sometimes well before daylight. Second best is in the evening, just before dark and even after dark.

Montana Fish, Wildlife & Parks even used sirens as part of a study on coyotes in the central portion of the state. They used sirens at a constant level, between eleven at night and five in the morning. They'd count coyotes that would answer back.

I have had coyotes respond to a siren and actually come toward it. That may sound good, but it can ruin some setups for you. If they come in and you're not ready for them, they'll spot you and simply become educated to be siren-shy.

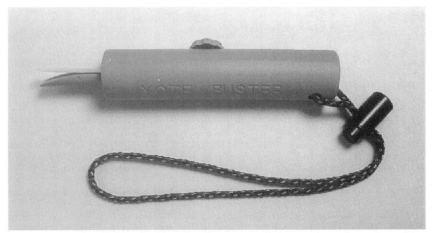

An open-reed call, like the Yote Buster, can produce a variety of sounds and is especially well suited for callers during the cold months of winter.

Chapter Two ■

What I like to do sometimes is to come through an area before daylight and locate different groups of coyotes with the siren. Then I can mentally mark them down, or mark them down on a map, and come back after the sun is up and hunt them. That way I'll have located my hunting spots and know that there are coyotes in those areas.

If you don't have a siren, that doesn't mean you can't locate coyotes before you try calling to them. You can get coyotes to answer back to a howler, too. The howler doesn't carry as far as a siren would, but it will sometimes get an answer.

If you do use sirens in an area, you may have to check with local authorities to make sure there isn't any law against using them.

As to the coyote calls you might use, there are two basic types—internal mouth calls and open- or closed-reed calls. Both have their pros and cons. As to my personal preference, I like the open-reed calls. My reason is that these calls

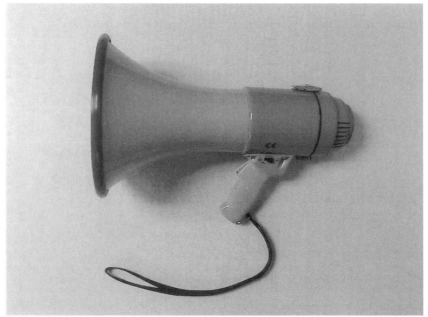

Portable, hand-held sirens are a relatively new tool for coyote hunters.
A siren allows you to locate coyotes when you're away from your vehicle.

allow you to make a great variety of sounds—to howl, make rabbit-in-distress sounds, or make canine-in-distress sounds. Why open-reed over closed-reed? Closed-reed calls work fine in warmer weather, but can freeze up when you get moisture in them during cold weather. Also, you're limited to whatever sound the closed-reed call is set up to make. If you use a closed-reed call, you've got to pack other calls along to make the other sounds.

My own call, the Yote Buster, became my favorite because it makes five different sounds that I use when I call in coyotes. It eliminates the need to pack along four other calls and still achieves the same results.

My own elk bugle, the Power Bugle, also works as a pretty good howler. In fact, it's one of the best, but it's really an elk bugle.

There are also mechanical calls. They are very popular. All you have to do is plug in a tape and turn on the machine. You never have to learn to call yourself. The drawback is that you're stuck with carrying extra batteries. They're bulky, and you have to take the time to set them out.

Finally, there's the squeaker call. You need one in your arsenal. It will amaze you how far away a coyote can hear little squeaks. Sometimes, I'll start using mine when the coyote is still out there two hundred yards. It doesn't matter. When a coyote hears that sound, it's often the deciding factor that brings him the rest of the way in.

The bottom line with all calls—except perhaps for the mechanical calls—is to practice with them. Take the time to learn how to use them. Then go out and call in some coyotes to make sure they work for you.

Other Stuff

Range finders—One of the newer gadgets that coyote hunters are packing along with them into the field these days is the optical range finder. These range finders calculate the yardage from the hunter to a distant object—sometimes a coyote. While that may sound handy, my impression is that they're not as helpful in hunting situations as you might imagine.

The problem with range finders is that it takes time to work them. They generally involve some movement. As a result, about the only time you can use them is when you make long shots at coyotes that have hung up in a calling sequence or have bedded down.

On the other hand, you might find a use for a range finder in other ways. They can be a good tool in training sessions. Guess the yardage to a distant object, then use the range finder to see if you were right or wrong. After you've shot a coyote, use the range finder to calculate the distance of your shot—that'll save you pacing off the distance.

But in actual hunting situations, most of the time you'll be too busy to use one.

Camo or white tape or cloth—Paying attention to the little details can sometimes reap big dividends for you. For example, pay attention to the glint and glare that sunlight can bounce off your equipment.

Some hunters use camouflage tape or cloth at times of no snow, and white tape or cloth when there is snow, to wrap their rifles and rifle scopes. The sun bouncing off a shiny surface can tip off an incoming coyote to a hunter that's up ahead of him.

If there was ever a time to justify two rifles, it's when you can have one that's covered in camouflage and another that's taped white. Sometimes I'll also use veterinarian wrap—used to wrap horse's legs—which doesn't stick to anything except itself. It comes in white or brown.

As you put your equipment together, pay attention to other items that might need a camo or white covering—or need to be concealed beneath your clothing. Those items include belt buckles, watches, binoculars, shooting sticks, and eyeglasses.

Maps—Without maps, you're lost in coyote country. Also, understand that maps serve more than one purpose for you. They give you the type of terrain you're looking at. They also give you most of the roads and trails and access points into and out of that country.

There are many extra things you can bring along on a coyote hunt.
The question is how many of them will be useful to you in locating a coyote.
Jim Hamilton photo.

Before you head out on a coyote-hunting trip, stop in at the local USDA Forest Service, Bureau of Land Management, or state agency that would have maps of that area. Take some time to study those maps. And be sure to take the maps along with you when you head into the area.

Cover scents—If there's an area in bad need of more research in terms of basic equipment, it's the use of cover scents. In the past, hunters didn't use them much. Somewhere along the line, as more pressure is put on coyotes, as these coyotes get smarter, and as you start to hunt more educated coyotes, cover scent will be one of the things that you turn to.

Out here in the West, where the area is so wide open, perhaps cover scent isn't necessary. But in areas of the East, or elsewhere in thicker habitat, cover scent might be an aid because coyotes have to come in so much closer before they're seen.

Also, short-range weapons—like muzzleloaders, handguns, or archery equipment—might make the use of cover scent more worthwhile.

Chapter Two ■

A length of rope will help you drag a coyote so you don't wind up being covered with fleas. A rope also comes in handy if you hang the coyote up for skinning to get the pelt.

Skinning gear—Pack along a small rope. It can be used for dragging coyotes, to keep the fleas off of you. If you plan on skinning your coyote out on the prairie, you can use the rope to hang the coyote. I use a Yote Tote that we developed for dragging and skinning. Another thing to note is that if you're skinning a coyote, it also doesn't hurt to bring along some latex gloves. To kill the fleas, a plastic sack is handy. You can put the coyote in a plastic sack and then spray it with flea-killing insect spray.

Sitting pad—If you're going to be sitting on stand, a little cushioned pad or a small carpet sample can be handy indeed. They can protect you from cactus spikes. They can also keep your rump dry if there's snow on the ground, if it is wet with rain, or if it is covered with dew.

Notebook—While it may seem like an extra thing you wouldn't need, a notebook can be another valuable tool to a coyote hunter. In that notebook, keep a careful record of what happened, what responded to the call, what call was used, whether you harvested a male or female, the date, and the time. If you go back into that area to call again, you can find out what you used, if it worked, and what you might try.

I'll call three hundred or four hundred areas and setups in a single year. No matter how good your memory might be, you can't remember them all. And all it takes is a little notebook to help refresh your memory and make you a more effective coyote hunter.

Chapter Two ■

CHAPTER THREE

EXAMINING COYOTE COUNTRY

I asked a buddy once where he had recently caught an awfully nice stringer of fish. The friend tugged at his mustache, scratched his head, and told me.

"It's a real easy fishing hole to find," he began.

"You go down the road a couple of miles.

"Then you turn right when you see a couple of cows in a field.

"Go a couple of more miles, then turn left when you see a horse.

"Drive a few more miles until you get to the top of a big hill.

"If you step out of your vehicle right there and squint your eyes just so, you can almost see that fishing hole."

Puzzled, I asked him, "What if I don't see a couple of cows, or the horse has been moved to another pasture, or I stop on the wrong hilltop, or I don't squint my eyes just so?"

The friend just laughed, "If that's the case, you're in the wrong spot. You'll just have to find that fishing hole for yourself."

And so it goes with coyote hunting. This chapter may be called "Examining Coyote Country," but the truth of the matter is that you're going to have to find your coyote-hunting spots for yourself.

What we'll try to do, however, is to give you some clues, some hints, some generalities on where to look to find those spots for yourself. Although coyotes inhabit a wide variety of places, a coyote is still a coyote.

Our goals here aren't so much to tell you about turning right, turning left, looking for cows or horses, but to give you a running start in looking at coyote country with better-informed eyes. When you see the things we'll talk about here, you'll have a better chance of finding that coyote and setting yourself up in a position to successfully call him in.

Getting Started

Coyote country is often big country. In the East, there are often big blocks of forestland. In the West, you see miles and miles—and miles—of open country. Trying to figure out where to start coyote hunting is a matter of taking these big blocks of land and analyzing them, picking them apart, looking for the various portions of that country most likely to hold a coyote.

Like every other creature in this world, the coyote has preferences. It has places that are more congenial. It has portions of habitat that it inhabits more often than other portions.

In the West, where we hunt, cover is often a critical concern. Big blocks of wheat stubble don't offer much security for a coyote. Neither do grazed-down pastures. Nor do big, barren flats. When I first started hunting coyotes, for example, one tip that really helped me was to look to winter pastures, areas where the grass tended to be taller because it was being saved for the cold months of the year. Invariably, those winter pastures held more coyotes than areas that had been heavily grazed.

Terrain can be a critical concern. Look for rugged country adjacent to those wheat fields. In that rugged country, a coyote can find a place to hide. Look to little valleys, coulees, and draws that cut into a pasture and offer a little

Coyote country is really big country in the West. You've got to do your homework to sort out the best areas where you can find and call coyotes.

brush or tall grass, where a coyote can take a day-long nap without being spotted.

Water can make a difference for coyotes. If it's an arid portion of the West, that water source is important during denning time and on through the summer and fall. It can act as a magnet for coyote movements across a wide area. And even in the East, creek bottoms often become travel routes, in addition to providing water for coyotes and other creatures.

Always, food is a major factor in determining coyote distribution. Prairie dog towns always attract predators like the coyote. Rugged country where desert cottontails tend to gather will draw coyotes looking for a meal. Grassy areas where rodents are abundant will produce coyotes. So will marshy spots because of the number of creatures that live in them. And if you know where deer or antelope drop fawns, those areas will also attract coyotes.

By analyzing the needs of a coyote and applying those needs to the terrain, you can get started in figuring out where you want to begin. You can start the filtering process that weeds out the unproductive areas and gets you closer to the places most likely to hold coyotes. From there, you need to check into those spots a little further.

Reading Sign

After you've looked at the big picture and decided which general areas are likely to hold coyotes, it's time to strap on your hiking boots, grab your binoculars, and do a little leg-work to narrow down your search a little more.

A coyote's life is all about movement. Coyotes simply have to move to find food. It rarely comes to them. So the first places you need to look are the natural travel paths that deer make and the cow paths that cattle follow.

As anyone who has ever hunted in the mountains will tell you, there's a reason why deer or elk have beaten down those game trails. They are invariably the easiest way to negotiate the topography of the high country. In the open prairie, those game trails are situated so they traverse draws and coulees in the easiest way or lead to prime food sources. As for the cattle trails, they often lead to stock dams or other water holes or follow creek bottoms or stream courses.

All of these paths are potential travel routes for coyotes. Based on my experiences, the paths and trails that go through a saddle or divide, go around the end of a hill, or travel along a creek bottom where animals are funneled into a certain area are some of the best places to look.

If there is snow on the ground or it has rained recently, it's pretty easy to check those trails for coyote tracks. If there's enough snow on the ground, you can even check the trails from a distance with your binoculars. A coyote travels in a straight line more than a fox does, and its track is bigger than a fox's. If there's no snow or rain, you'll have to look more closely in the dirt and dust to read the signs that coyotes leave behind. But you can still read the sign.

With a little practice, you can identify the scat that coyotes leave behind. It's a bit different than that of a fox or bobcat.

And depending on how fresh it is, you can get a pretty good indication of how long ago a coyote passed that way.

When you find these signs, it's time to look at the country around you. Try to analyze where the coyotes might be coming from and where they might be going. Look for natural passes in the hills. Look for food sources they might be using. Look for areas where they might hole up during the day.

If food sources are abundant, you stand the chance of calling in several coyotes if you make a good setup. Abundant prey translates into abundant coyotes. With a lot of food, you can have quite a few coyotes in a small area. If food is scarce, the territories of individual coyotes will be much larger. There might just be that one animal that left the tracks or scat behind.

This ability to read sign and analyze the country around that sign is something that will get better and better with experience. The more you do it and the more success you find, the better you'll become.

When filming coyote videos, for example, I have to analyze the terrain where we make our setups. I need to know the likely travel paths that coyotes will take when they come in to a call. If I guess wrong, there'll be no film footage shot. In my early days with a camera, that was as likely as not to happen. But, as I said, you get better with practice. You look for the natural passes through the hills. You look for the trails that feed into an area. Eventually, you pick out the places where a coyote is likely to appear.

Sometimes, of course, you can get too good at picking out these kinds of spots. One time, I was hunting with a partner and we picked out a butte that stood out from all the rest. There was a creek nearby, and we were in a vehicle on one side of the creek. The butte was on the other. But we figured it looked like a pretty good spot, so we went over there and got ready to make a setup to call.

In our part of coyote country, one of your basic concerns when you make a setup is where you're going to sit down. There are a lot of cactus out there and if you sit in the wrong spot, you're not only going to feel some instant discomfort, but it's going to be awfully tough to pick out the spines, too.

Chapter Three ■

*By reading the tracks that coyotes leave behind, you can get an idea of travel
routes and determine the relative abundance of coyotes in the area.
Jim Hamilton photo.*

I was looking down for that prime sitting spot and figured I'd found it, when out of the corner of my eye, I spotted a coyote running down the hill. I immediately raised my rifle and pointed it at the spot. To my partner, that was like a signal that something must be there. I don't usually just unsling my rifle and point it that quickly.

Both of us started shooting at the coyote. And both of us missed it. But later, based on the coyote's tracks, we saw that he was thirteen steps from where I was going to sit down when I spotted him. And it was five steps from my sitting spot to where he had been bedded down.

Another example of how important it is to analyze coyote country was provided by a friend of mine who is an avid coyote caller and very successful at it. I asked him his secret of success. He told me that, for him, it was very important to find travel routes.

Normally, a coyote caller will only stay at a place for a relatively short time. But sometimes my friend would sit there and call for an hour to two hours in a single setup. His success ratio was so high because he was willing to sit alongside that well-used travel route for a long time, knowing that sooner or later, a coyote was going to come by.

How successful was he as a coyote caller? If my friend used about ten setups, he'd be successful at about six of them. That's an exceedingly high percentage. But he had learned his country exceedingly well. And every spot he tried was exceedingly good at producing coyotes.

Places to Look

Where do you look for coyotes? You look in the places that provide the best chance of finding a coyote. It's just that simple.

Coyote habitat consists of a food source and reasonable cover. If you find these ingredients together, there should be coyotes. If you have great food and great cover, you've got the potential for a great coyote-hunting spot. If one part of the equation or the other isn't quite so good, the potential for the coyote-hunting spot will suffer as well.

Chapter Three ■

With that in mind, one of my favorite areas is around grain stubble fields where there are adjacent brushy draws, small tree patches, or plum thickets. There are often rabbits or mice associated with the grain fields themselves or the nearby brush. I like to call into the rough country or the cover adjacent to the stubble fields. Those kinds of places tend to hold a lot of coyotes. In North and South Dakota, Wyoming, and Montana, it's common to find those fields on plateaus, with rough country that's unsuitable for farming somewhere around them. To me, that's a sure combination for coyotes.

Prairie dog towns are a strong attraction for coyotes. Once again, they're a solid food base. If you're in an area with prairie dog towns, spend some time in the early morning with your binoculars, glassing the town. If there are draws or coulees in the area, spend some time there looking for tracks and security cover. Often coyotes will hunt the towns, then spend their daylight hours bedded down in the nearby cover.

Ask any sheep rancher, and he'll tell you that sheep tend to attract coyotes, especially at lambing time. It goes without saying that very few sheep ranchers will balk at coyote hunters trying their luck on calling in sheep country. But cattle seem to attract coyotes as well, especially in winter. Where ranchers are feeding livestock, the coyotes will come in and eat cow manure for the protein in the feed that's still in the manure. The manure apparently supplements their diet in winter when it's cold. When ranchers gather livestock to calve in the spring, coyotes will come into those areas and feed on the afterbirth of the cows as well as on newborn calves.

In our part of the world, we have a lot of badland areas. When you look at them, you wouldn't think that anything could survive out there, except maybe a jackrabbit. But the truth is that badlands tend to produce a lot of coyotes. They typically have a sprinkling of cedars, plateaus, isolated areas of good grass. These areas hold a lot of cottontail rabbits, some jackrabbits, deer, and mice. The coyotes feel comfort-

When it catches the early morning light, the coat of a coyote tends to light up, making him easier to spot. That's why it's best to look for coyotes with the sun at your back. Jim Hamilton photo.

able in the broken country. As a result, badlands are great places to hunt for coyotes.

Look for the most obvious travel routes. Like all animals, coyotes tend to use the easiest routes in their daily travels. They're not going to travel in the really rough stuff unless they have to. Funnel areas in creek valleys are one place to look. Areas of cover between big openings are another. Fence lines tend to restrict coyote movement. And coyotes like to go through open gates—especially in sheep country where there are sheep-tight fences.

Some coyote areas are seasonal. In the spring of the year, one of the best places to look is near water. Coyotes like to pick den sites where there's a ready source of water nearby. Look for coyote sign leading to and from the water source. Look for good cover in the area. If you scan these areas closely enough, you'll find either the den site or the coyotes themselves.

We do have some big areas of timber in coyote country, even in the West. But calling coyotes in the timber limits your ability to see very far. Timber also muffles the sound of your calling. The general feeling in this part of the coyote world is that, unless something is drastically wrong in the other calling areas, we prefer not to call in the timber. And, in truth, I've never had a lot of luck calling in timber country. Coyotes don't like to come across an open field when there's timber all around it. They'd rather stay in the timber. As a result, there's no doubt in my mind that, under the cover of that timber, many of the coyotes I've called have probably circled downwind—and got my scent—and I never even knew there was a coyote in the area.

A friend of mine had an experience that would seem to lend some credence to those feelings. He spotted a group of coyotes across a huge opening in the timber and figured he'd have easy pickings calling them in. There was so much open space between him and them and the clearing was so large, he thought they'd most certainly come right at him.

He started to call and saw them start coming across the opening, then drop into a low spot. After that, he didn't see them again. But after a while, as he continued to call, he no-

Coyotes' coloration helps them blend into the background, which is why it's easier to spot them out in the open rather than in brush or in the forest. Jim Hamilton photo.

ticed a movement off to the side of him in the timber. There were the coyotes, checking him out. Rather than come across the opening, they took a less direct route toward the source of the calling. That route, however, kept them in the security cover that the timber provided. My friend never got an open shot.

If you are restricted to timber country, my best advice is to pick areas that are as open as possible. Your calls will carry farther. You'll stand a better chance of spotting coyotes before they spot you or catch your wind. Look to power line clearcuts, logged-over areas, abandoned roads, ice-covered marshes, anywhere you can get an unrestricted line of vision for a long distance. Realize, too, that learning exact travel routes of coyotes and working those routes will be even more important because, in timbered country, you have to be so much closer for coyotes to hear your calls.

Once again, learning your coyote country and reading the signs will help you make the most of all the other skills that go into coyote hunting.

Get Some Help

If there's a rugged individualist in the hunting world, it must be the coyote hunter. And it seems coyote hunters are heavy into the strong, silent types as well. They'd just as soon discover everything on their own. They are more prone than other hunters to keep their information to themselves. And it seems the more successful they are, the less they are likely to socialize about it. Like I said—strong, silent, rugged, individualist.

But hey, if you're looking for good coyote spots, it never hurts to talk to others a bit. After all, others might have some information that will speed the process of examining coyote country. They can offer some leads as to good places to hunt. They can shorten the process of unraveling the puzzle of where coyotes go and what they do.

The most logical people you need to talk to are the farmers and ranchers who live out among the coyotes. Stop in and talk to the landowners. You'll find that probably 95 percent

*By talking to ranchers, farmers, wardens, and biologists, you can narrow your
search area and get a good idea of where coyotes are hiding.
Jim Hamilton photo.*

of them will be happy that you stopped in and will be happy to let you hunt coyotes. There are going to be a few who don't want people shooting coyotes on their property. They might not like people on their property at all. But you'll find that most ranchers will not only let you hunt coyotes, they'll be happy to share their knowledge of where they've seen coyotes, the food that coyotes are keying on, and where the most likely cover areas for coyotes might be.

Game wardens and other fish and game personnel can help you and give you leads on where they've seen a lot of coyotes. These people are often in the field every day, and some cover huge territories. They also talk to more hunters in the course of their jobs than you or I would ever get a chance to meet. Use them as a source.

Area gun shops and sporting goods dealers might offer you still other insights, including some that might surprise you. The worst news they can give you is that there are a lot of active coyote hunters in the area. If that's the case, your calling in that country probably isn't going to be as successful as if there were few coyote hunters. Inevitably, your best success will be in areas that are more remote and less heavily hunted.

The bottom line with all this socialization is to get an idea of how many coyotes there are in a particular area and get some leads on where those coyotes might be. If there are a lot of callers around, for example, you'll find that a lot of them are calling off the main roads. They'll call a drainage, then move on. If you follow in their tracks, you'll end up with a lot of setups and not many coyotes to show for it.

If there are a lot of coyotes around and not too many coyote hunters, you can expect better success. If there aren't many coyotes out there or a lot of hunters are out after them, you won't call in many. It's just that simple.

Reasonable Expectations

I don't care how good a coyote caller you are. I don't care how good the coyote country might be. The bottom line is that you're not going to call in a coyote every time you make a setup and every time you call.

What are reasonable expectations?

If you call in a coyote once in every four or five stands, that's a good average.

If you call in a coyote three times out of ten stands, that's an A-plus.

You don't always call a coyote in on every stand.

That's why it's so important to examine coyote country and pick your setups wisely. By setup, what I mean is picking the places you choose to call. Playing the wind right is important. Having enough information and sign to expect that coyotes use that particular area. Knowing that there are enough coyotes in the area that you stand a good chance of calling one in.

It's not just a matter of stopping anywhere and tooting on a call. In fact, you're better off to make three good stands in coyote country than ten bad stands. Your success ratio will improve dramatically.

In the different calling setups we do, it's important to think like a coyote when you're looking at coyote country. During the middle of the day, most of the time, you should know that coyotes are going to be in some type of cover. You should look at their feeding areas and know that those with cover are probably going to be the most productive. You should look for the winter pastures, the adjacent stubble or cutover cornfields where mice and other rodents will be abundant, the rugged drainages where coyotes will hole up during the day.

The closer you get to these better spots, the better off you are. Calls will travel some distance, if you get close enough. But you've got to get that close. If you make a good stand in good country, your chances are better than making a poor stand in good country, or any stand at all in country that doesn't have many coyotes.

Also, you've got to be willing to put in the time it takes to find the good spots. There have been days when we've wasted a whole morning without making a setup. We've started early with our howling or with a siren and kept it up for half the day. We'd simply locate coyotes. Then we'd

*You don't always call a coyote in at every stand, and in open country,
the stands might be a long walk in between.*

take our maps and make our marks, knowing that we could
work those areas in the afternoon or in other days ahead.

How important is it to have a good setup with plenty of
coyotes in the area? Let me tell it this way.

We were calling one time in the mountains and spotted a
coyote way off on a high mountain peak. It was early in the
morning, and when you have the sun at your back, their
hide glistens in that light. They're pretty easy to spot.

We figured that considering where that coyote was, and
with the country in between, we probably couldn't get any
closer. So we started calling right there. I'll be honest. We
never called that coyote in. But in between us and the coyote, there was a hayfield with some cattle in it. After we
started calling, we looked through our binoculars and spotted another coyote that we hadn't seen—and it was coming
in toward us.

As coyotes sometimes do, he was hunting his way toward
us. They do that, hunt their way in. This particular coyote
jumped a group of sharp-tailed grouse in that hayfield.
When they flushed, the coyote jumped up and caught one in
midair. He stopped right there and ate him. We continued

Chapter Three ■

calling while he ate his morning meal. And when he got done eating, here he came. Even after eating that bird, he came right in when we called him.

In the end, there's no substitute for doing your homework and your legwork in coyote country. You've got to have a reasonable idea of how many coyotes are in the area and where they're likely to be. At that point, you can start putting things together so that all your other tactics can come into play.

Once you start recognizing where the coyotes are and where they're likely to appear, it all starts to come together. It's like a big puzzle. And when you put it all together, you'll start finding success as a coyote hunter.

CHAPTER FOUR

BASIC TECHNIQUES

It's a simple case of following four P's—proper preparation for peak performance. That's the case in so many things in life. It's the same in becoming a good coyote hunter.

You prepare yourself by learning about the animals themselves. You prepare by putting together good basic equipment. Then you do your homework on the area you plan to hunt. You do some map work, some talking to others, some legwork reading sign and evaluating the various places where you might make a setup.

While all these things may not seem quite as exciting as taking your stand, pulling out your coyote calls, and making some music on them, believe me when I tell you that they provide the sound foundation for all coyote hunting.

If you short yourself by avoiding any of these tasks, your success in the coyote game is going to suffer. If you make these vital preparations, then you're ready to move onto the next step.

It's time to go hunting and start putting that homework to good use. It's time to head out and start calling in coyotes.

The Time

Coyote hunters tend to be early risers—and for good reason. The best time to locate, spot, and call coyotes is early in the morning. Coyotes typically hunt at night and into the prime hours of predawn and just postdawn.

Depending on the type of day and the time of year, that prime hunting period may extend three to four hours after sunrise.

Again, you have to think like a coyote to maximize your opportunities. Pay attention to how you are feeling, as well.

For example, the calling period after dawn is much shorter during the summer. When the sun is up for a while and it starts to get too warm for you, rest assured that it's getting too warm for that coyote wearing his fur coat. When a coyote starts to feel that warmth, it looks for a shaded piece of cover where it can bed for the day and make itself as comfortable as possible.

During the summer months, coyotes may stay in that piece of cool cover all day long and be reluctant to leave it. And why should they? It's hot out there. Food is most plentiful during the summer months, with all those prey species having their young. To lure a coyote out of his bed, you're going to have to be very close and sound very enticing.

As a result, many coyote hunters take the tactic of following suit. They do their locating and calling in the early morning, then take a nap themselves during the day. There's no point in fighting nature.

During fall and especially during winter, both coyotes and coyote hunters tend to be more active during longer portions of the day. Hunting is tougher for coyotes. Prey isn't quite so abundant, and the young of the year that have survived have grown smarter. Coyotes are also burning more calories just keeping themselves warm.

That tends to stretch out the coyote's active period to more hours past sunrise. Their daylong bedding turns into

Coyotes tend to be more active during the winter months because food sources are less abundant and they need more calories to stay warm. Jim Hamilton photo.

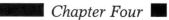 Chapter Four ■

more of a series of short naps. Coyotes that were unsuccessful at getting game during the night are forced to hunt more during the day. At times, they may hunt all day long. As a result, coyote hunters may find that they can be successful all day long.

Early morning has yet another advantage for the coyote hunter that becomes readily apparent when you start hunting the hours of evening, the second most productive time of the day. In the morning, you're in a situation of gathering light. The longer you're out there in the predawn, dawn, and postdawn period, the lighter it gets. That means when you're working a coyote, you don't have to worry that light conditions are going to ruin your setup just when a coyote is coming in.

In the evening, hunting tends to get better and better the later it gets. Coyotes become increasingly active as darkness approaches. The darkness also offers a sense of security to coyotes. They know they're safer in times of darkness. The darkness cloaks their actions and gives them an advantage over their prey and against other predators—like you. They may not be able to see as well in the gloom of evening, but they can still see better than you can.

One time during one of those evening setups, we were walking to our last calling spot when we bumped a coyote. It was about 4 p.m., and he had been lying down in a grassy spot in the bottom of a draw. As the coyote took off, we couldn't get a shot at him. But we watched him, and he ran into the next draw and disappeared.

With one coyote in the area and time slipping away on us, we figured we might just as well get a position up high and try calling to see if there was another one nearby. Soon after we set up and began calling, a second coyote appeared, running up a long draw toward us. He kept running, and running, and running, and finally he ran right past us. When he got out a little ways, he must have spotted us because he spooked a bit. We gave a call on a squeaker, and the coyote stopped and looked back. That's where we dropped him.

With so little time left in the day, there was no time to make another setup, so we let things settle for a time, then started calling again. After a short time, here came a third coyote from another direction. This coyote came in to a distance of about a quarter mile from us, then started mousing. That coyote moused and moused. No matter what call we tried, he wouldn't come in any farther.

Time was slipping away from us. There was still enough light for shooting, but for a full half-hour, we couldn't seem to budge that coyote from chasing mice. Just when it appeared that fading daylight would end the opportunity, the coyote stopped chasing mice and continued to come toward us. He came in on a path that would take him near where we had dropped the second coyote. And when he smelled the blood of that coyote, he stopped. That's where we dropped him, too.

The Setup

Just as the timing of your hunting is important, so is the setup. By that I mean how you approach the stand where you plan to call, how you pick out the stand, what you do and don't do. It also means knowing when everything is right for calling and when things aren't right (and you decide to slip out of the area rather than make a setup that's bound to end in failure or, worse yet, simply educate coyotes to avoid callers there in the future).

Probably the thing that coyote hunters have to realize the most is that they're just that—hunters. Every minute they're out there getting ready to take a stand and call, they have to act as if the hunt is on. They have to act as if things will go sour because they've tipped off a coyote unnecessarily. They've got to take an attitude that they're stalking game.

To begin with, it means that you're probably not going to be able to drive right up to your stand. Automobiles make noise. Headlights in the predawn are a sure sign of man invading coyote country. So you need to take some care with your driving approach. If you can, drive into an area with your headlights off. Park your vehicle a half mile or more

An animal silhouetted on the skyline is easily spotted by the hunter.
A hunter silhouetted on the skyline is easily spotted by animals, too.
Jim Hamilton photo.

away. Get out of your vehicle quietly. Begin your stalk from the time you leave the highway.

With that in mind, how do you approach your stand? I think that's where a lot of people make their biggest mistakes. People spend too much time on the skyline looking around. They spend too much time glassing up there. They spend too much time talking with their partners up there. They make themselves visible for far too long.

You need to get off those skylines quickly, to use the terrain to try to hide your profile, so you're not silhouetted up there. When I come into a calling stand, I come in crouched, with a low profile, and I come in quickly and quietly and sit down. I'm not standing and looking around, giving the animal a chance to observe me.

If I have to sit down quickly in a spot that isn't the ideal spot, I'll do it. Then I'll look around and move to another spot nearby, which might have more visibility and be a little more comfortable. In short, you literally hunt your way to your hunting spot.

When I leave the area, I try to do it in the same way that I came in. I'll get up quietly trying not to make sounds. I'll use the terrain to hide myself. I'll try not to skyline myself, or I'll skyline myself for as short a time as possible. Sneak in. Sneak out.

Whether you're successful or not, try to disturb the area as little as possible. Why? The reason you've come there in the first place is that, even if you haven't called in a coyote on this particular setup, your research has shown that the area has the potential to produce a coyote for you sometime. When you come back, you don't want to have to face coyotes that have identified you as a hunter by your previous mistakes.

That's the same reason why it's important that you know when not to call from a particular spot. You don't want to ruin it for some future time.

If you've located the coyotes and you can't use the terrain or the wind to your advantage, it's better to leave the area and come back at a later time—even if it's an hour or two later. To do otherwise will spoil the coyote and ruin the stand.

That's true even when I thought I was locating coyotes with a siren or by howling. Sometimes those coyotes come in when you're not ready. In situations like that, if you can't immediately go into a stand and call them, you're better off moving and coming back later.

It's time, too, to pay attention to environmental factors around you. Wind direction is one of the biggest factors you'll have to take into account when setting up a stand. If the wind is not in your favor, or if you can't keep an eye on the downwind side, you're better off not making a stand.

If the wind is blowing extremely hard, you can still call in coyotes, but your odds for a successful kill drop with every extra mile per hour that the wind is blowing. In strong winds, your scent is carried a long distance. Sometimes coyotes can smell you out to two or three hundred yards or even farther away. That their noses can be that sensitive still amazes me. But time after time, they pick up your scent far, far away in that wind. Once they pick up your scent, the game is probably over.

Keep in mind that the cardinal rule of calling is to cover your backside, cover your downwind side. Most of the time, a coyote will try to circle downwind to try to see if it's safe to come in or not. Rather than come straight in, they'll angle around to the downwind side. Always leave an open area downwind where you can get an animal stopped before he catches your wind. If you can't do that, it's best not to call there.

But let's say conditions are right. The wind is coming from the right direction. How do you go about making a setup to call in coyotes?

If I'm calling in the morning or evening, the first thing I'll do is pay attention to the sun. I'll try to find a location where the sun is at my back. That accomplishes two things for me. With the sun at my back, it's easier to glass and look for coyotes. The sunlight will light them up. And I won't have the glare of the sun to look into. If you sit in the shade of a hill and look into a sunlit area, that's also a good tactic. The hill will provide a good backdrop. It'll also be harder for the coyote to see into the shade and spot you.

Often, I'll sneak in over a ridgetop and sit down right away and glass the area a little bit. I'll look around and see if there are any coyotes within easy view. I'll also begin looking around for a better position. You might be sitting right out in the open on that first go-round. Then you move to the better spot.

In looking for that spot, I'll try to find a bit of cover to break up my outline. I'll look for a piece of brush, some heavy grass, some rocks, something to break up my outline. One of the nice things about using mouth calls is that you can move into these spots quickly and without much movement. You don't have to get up and put your speakers out, as you would with a mechanical call.

When you decide on your calling position, also make sure it's a comfortable spot. Figure that you're going to have to sit or lie there, basically motionless, for at least twenty minutes to a half-hour. While none of us wants to admit to aging, it seems the older you get, the harder it is to sit or lie in

If possible when you're calling, sit in the shade provided by small hills, rocks, trees, or brush and look out into the sunny areas.

one position for long periods without moving around. That's one reason why we've learned to always carry a pad to sit on. That makes sitting more comfortable. We also dress appropriately for the day. If it's going to be cold, we bundle up, especially making sure that our heads, hands, and feet stay warm. If it's going to be hot, we try to sit in the shade. Every creature comfort that you can provide for yourself is going to make it easier for you to sit still. And sitting still is critically important. Remember that those coyotes have keen eyesight. No matter how well you're camouflaged, movement can and will give away your presence.

Another thing to remember is that calling uphill is better than calling downhill. It's easier to call a coyote up to you from down below. In the badlands, that's relatively easy. You can set up in an uphill position. It increases your calling success because you have better visibility of the coyote coming in.

Second best is calling from the same elevation. If you're calling out on the flatlands, do the best you can to pick out some kind of cover and some kind of background that's going to break up your outline. That might be a fenceline where you can sit with your back to a post. It might be a haystack or a rock pile that provides a bit of cover and a slightly elevated position so you can see a bit better.

The worst scenario is when you set up in a position below the coyotes. In that case, your visibility suffers. Also, coyotes seem to like to come downhill to a caller less well.

As you sneak into your spot, remember one other thing. You're not the only creature out and about in coyote country. One of the creatures that you're sharing coyote country with is the rattlesnake.

Let me illustrate. One time I was hunting in fall. It had been cold early in the day, but the sun had come out, it had warmed up, and it turned into a beautiful morning. I was sitting on stand and thinking about how nice it would be to just put my hands behind my head, lie back, and soak up the sun a bit. I didn't do that. And it was a good thing I didn't.

When I put my hand down to boost myself up, a rattlesnake began buzzing. It turned out that the rattlesnake was just behind me. If I had laid back, he would have been about a foot from my elbow. I moved away and called to my partner, who was farther down the slope. Together, we looked at the rattler, which had about ten rattles on its tail. And we shot him before we moved on.

Another time, I was out with a friend and a dog, moving through coyote country on our way to a setup. This time, we had to walk between two big sagebrush. The dog walked through. I walked through. Then, when my friend walked through, I heard a pop. A rattlesnake had been under one of those sage plants. When my friend walked through, the snake struck at him, hitting the bottom of his shoe. He was only wearing low-top sneakers. My friend wasn't hurt. But it just goes to show that the first guy through isn't always the one who's going to know that there's a snake nearby. Often the first guy just awakens the snake and agitates it a bit. It can be the second guy who gets nailed.

Why go to all this painstaking bother to create a perfect setup before you ever put a call to your mouth? Put it all together, and you've overcome some of the coyote's formidable defenses, and you've tipped the scales at least a little bit in your favor.

If you've snuck into your spot, hopefully the coyote doesn't know you're there. If the coyote comes in, he'll be battling the glare of the sun in trying to see you. If you've figured the wind right, the coyote won't be able to smell you and will be in a position where you can get off a shot before he circles downwind. And if you can sit there, comfortable and motionless, for a long period of time, he shouldn't be able to pick up on your presence by spotting you.

Then you can begin calling.

Basic Calling

The questions I'm asked most often by novice coyote callers are how, how much, how loud, and how often do you call. They're fairly simple questions. But the answers aren't quite so easy. Calling doesn't always follow a basic recipe. It depends on the coyotes themselves and often has to be tailored to specific situations. As to loudness, the consensus among callers is that too much volume will hurt you. I tend to agree, but each situation is different and weather conditions often dictate whether you need to blow your calls with more or less volume.

When I settle into my calling position, I often sit there for a while. I won't start calling right away. Sometimes a coyote might be within view. If you can locate the coyote right away before you begin calling, you might change your calling technique. Some guys will start calling immediately, as soon as they sit down. I prefer not to. If you can locate your coyote before you start calling, your success rate will go up considerably. So I'll let the area settle down a bit. I'll do some glassing. I'll get myself prepared.

When I start calling, I like to call a series of three or four rabbit-in-distress calls in a minute. Then I wait for three to five minutes and see what happens. During that time, I'll be glassing with binoculars to see if anything is out there. It's also the time when I put the binoculars down to catch a

Of all the sounds you make, the basic rabbit-in-distress sound is the one that most often brings coyotes within range. Jim Hamilton photo.

glimpse of anything else that might be nearby or coming in from another direction.

If I don't see anything, I call again for one or two minutes. I'll repeat that sequence of calling, then stopping and glassing, three or four times. That will cover anywhere from fifteen to twenty minutes. In fact, most coyotes will respond in the first five to ten minutes. If there's a coyote in the area, that's how quickly it'll most likely come in.

One other thing I'll do is start out my calling sequence with a softer series of calls. That way, if there's a coyote nearby, I won't be hollering in his ear. If I get no response on those softer calls, then I start adding volume to my other calling sequences to reach out a little farther.

If I get a response and a coyote begins coming in, I'll adjust the volume of my calling. I don't need to always operate at maximum volume. I'll also be able to go to the squeaker when he gets within listening range of that call. That's the advantage of both being able to see the coyotes coming in and to using a mouth call rather than an electronic one. Most of those electronic calls operate at the same volume, or you have to make movements to adjust them. With mouth calls and squeakers, you can adjust your calling more easily.

If no coyotes come in, I'll wait a little while in my calling spot to see if something is still coming in. You don't just get up and leave. And when you do decide to move out, you do it quickly and quietly, as if you'd never been there.

Let me use an example of a basic calling sequence to show you how it works—or at least how it can work when it does work. One of the nice things about shooting video footage of coyote-hunting experiences is that it's pretty easy to reconstruct what happened on a particular hunting trip. All you have to do is look at your video footage.

All the sounds I used in this particular setup were rabbit-in-distress calls. That's pretty common, too. It was a winter calling sequence, and it involved calling to a fairly large area with a barren flat down below us, little hills, some rocks, and sagebrush, with timbered country off to both sides. It was about a mile and a half from a major river.

Chapter Four ■

We got into position and made our setup. Then I started with a soft rabbit-in-distress call. I blew the call no longer than a minute, then I stopped. I waited for about five minutes—and sometimes it's kind of handy to have a watch with you to space these calls out—as we glassed the country below us.

I called again with a loud rabbit-in-distress sound. At that point, through our binoculars, we spotted four coyotes about a mile and a half in the distance. I blew those loud rabbit sounds for about two minutes. We waited again, but this time only about three minutes, then hit the rabbit sounds again.

At that point, two of the four coyotes broke away and started coming toward us. I did the loud rabbit-in-distress because they were still so far out. As they approached, they stopped about a half mile out and I hit the loud rabbit-in-distress again. I blew it for about another minute, then I stopped. At that, the coyotes started coming until they stopped about two hundred yards out from us and just sat there. They were looking for where the sound was coming from, trying to pinpoint the location of that distressed rabbit.

A soft breeze was blowing from my right to my left. With the coyotes just two hundred yards out, I hit the squeaker and squeaked for about thirty seconds. One of the coyotes began toward us again, but with the rolling terrain of the hills, he dropped out of sight. I hit the squeaker one more time, and the second coyote started coming and also dropped out of sight.

We suspected—and correctly so—that the first coyote was trying to circle downwind to catch our scent. If he had followed the path we suspected, he wouldn't have been visible until he was above us. We sat tight and waited for two minutes without being able to see either coyote, figuring that soon one or the other would pop up somewhere nearby.

We had to do something, especially if that first coyote was circling downwind. If we waited too long, that coyote would catch our scent and be gone. I hit a medium distress sound, blowing it about three or four times. On the video, you can see the head of that first coyote peek over a hill about seventy yards away. All that are visible are his nose, eyes, and ears.

I hit the squeaker again—just a few squeaks. He ran up the hill on our left about twenty-five yards and stopped, almost at the point where he could have caught our scent. We dropped him right there.

Even after the shot, we didn't talk. We were still hunting for that second coyote. At a time like this, the sound to make is a canine-in-distress sound. You do it two, or three, or four times, and it will sometimes bring that second coyote in. This time it didn't work. It often does. If that canine-in-distress sound isn't in your calling repertoire, then go back to the basic rabbit-in-distress call. Sometimes that works, too. The second coyote will come in to see what's going on.

If you stick with this type of basic calling sequence, you'll have some success in coyote hunting. The key to it is tailoring your sounds to coyotes you can see, adjusting the type of call and volume to the distance of the animal. If the coyote is coming in, you don't need to call. If the coyote stops, or seems to lose its sense of where the call is coming from, you get on the call again to keep it coming.

In this type of calling sequence, you can also see why it's so important that all the other ingredients of your setup are in place: that you're calling from an elevated position, that you have good visibility all around, that you're able to see and shoot in the downwind direction, and that you're able to be comfortable and patient on your stand.

Finally, be serious. Have faith in your setup. Have faith in your calling. If not for this time on the setup, do it for the next time you're in the area.

After a little time of no action, some guys sometimes tend to start talking, or whistling, or singing, or carrying on. Maybe there is a coyote out there that hung up, or didn't come in, or simply lost interest. Maybe it's a coyote that you never even saw.

Don't get in the habit of slinging lead at a coyote that you know you really can't hit. Blazing away with a rifle at a running coyote isn't going to increase your success.

Chapter Four

If you tip that coyote off to your calling by letting him associate calling sounds with a hunter, you may never bring him in the next time you're in the area. It's only going to educate another coyote. It certainly isn't going to contribute to your success.

The key to basic coyote-hunting techniques is to follow the process and pay attention to the little things. Learn about the animals, the country they live in, and where they're found in that country. Then be effective in making your setup and carrying out your calling sequence. These are the building blocks of your foundation as a coyote hunter. They're the things you can build on to become a successful coyote hunter anywhere.

CHAPTER FIVE
ADVANCED TACTICS

You've got the basics now. You know how to start. It's time to get those all-important details worked out. In almost everything, it's paying attention to the details that separates the people who are pretty good at something from the ones who are very, very good at it.

It's also in paying attention to the details that coyote hunters can enjoy some of their greatest discoveries. They add pieces to the coyote-hunting puzzle. They observe something that tweaks their memory. They pick up clues that guide them to their next move in a difficult calling situation.

In this chapter, we're going to cover a lot of ground. We're going to scattergun out a whole lot of tactics. Some sections will be long ones. Others will be short. What we're trying to do here isn't so much provide you with a pat recipe for success, but to give you a base of knowledge on a lot of different things. It's an effort to expose you to many different aspects of coyote hunting, how to make setups, what you're likely to encounter after you've done your homework, your scouting, and you get into actual calling situations. If you're an experienced coyote hunter, you may know much of this already. If not, you'll quickly get an education.

The goal is to provide many different things that will tweak your memory when you get into the field. It's to tell you these things so that when you try them, or simply experience them, you'll say, "Okay, now I know what those guys were talking about. Now I know what to do."

One, Two, Three

Making a stand as an individual or calling with a friend, the scenario would be the same. But if you have more than two people making a stand, as people say, you might just as well have a beer party. With so many people, you can't camouflage everybody. You can't control everybody's movements.

Everybody wants to be part of the calling sequence. That's the name of the game. That's the fun. But it becomes very difficult to call in a coyote when there are more than two people involved.

Speaking from my own experience, that's one of the problems I've always had with filming. The two people I'd be filming would be the proper number. I became the third wheel. As a result, I was given the position where the caller would have sat, or the shooter would have sat, simply because I needed the good visibility to do the filming. That has ruined more than a few setups for us.

That's why we strongly advocate just working in pairs. It's not that you can't call coyotes in alone. Or even that you can't call coyotes in when more than two people are present. You most certainly can. But there's something to be said for one guy having a partner, somebody to share your experiences with, somebody to do the calling when you're the shooter and somebody to do the shooting when you're the caller.

But anytime you get more than two people involved, your problems compound geometrically with each additional person you add to the group.

The more people you bring along on a coyote-hunting trip, the more potential you have for a coyote to spot you. Two hunters is probably the ideal number. Jim Hamilton photo.

Chapter Five ■

Playing The Wind

When it's time to make a setup for calling, I like to advance into my calling area working into the wind. In fact, it's not just calling into the wind, but moving from stand to stand into the wind.

If you do it this way, then everything you call downwind is behind you. The majority of the time you'll be calling into an area that hasn't heard your sounds yet. If you do it the opposite way, working downwind, you don't know how far your sound is carrying. You might be working coyotes that have already heard you and decided not to come in. Calling to them is pretty much a waste of time because they didn't come in the last time they heard you.

As the wind comes up and gets stronger, you make your stands closer together. Your sounds don't travel as far into stronger winds.

When you do this, you can't ignore the area downwind of you, of course. A coyote might come in from that direction. Or a coyote from the upwind side might circle you and you won't see him until he's downwind.

How far apart should you make your stands? Again, that's a matter of wind strength. If the wind isn't too strong, my stands might be a mile apart. As the wind gets stronger, I might cut that distance to a half mile.

Playing the wind this way, you might cover only five or six miles of good coyote country on a day with stronger winds. On a windless day, you might cover the same ground in three or four setups. Wind is the determining factor.

One time, a friend from South Dakota came out to hunt coyotes with me. That day, the wind was blowing twenty-five to thirty miles per hour. Normally, I wouldn't have even hunted. But since he came from far away, we decided to give it a try.

Surprisingly, we called several coyotes in that day. The next day the wind was blowing fifty to sixty miles per hour. We stayed home. It would have been a waste of

When it's windy, coyotes tend to be more wary and sounds don't travel as far. But if you wait for a windless day in the West, you won't be hunting very often. Jim Hamilton photo.

Chapter Five ■

time. Ideally, I don't like the wind to be more than about fifteen miles per hour.

Wind affects the ability of coyotes to hear and pinpoint the source of sounds. Wind seems to break the call up. At a distance, coyotes can't seem to tell exactly where the sound is coming from. That makes your calling less effective.

Higher wind speeds also seem to affect the behavior of coyotes. They're not comfortable. They're more nervous coming in. They're more excitable, more jumpy. It seems to put them on edge and makes them more wary. It makes them tougher to call.

On the other hand, if you decide to hunt coyotes only on windless, or relatively windless, days, you won't be doing much hunting in our part of the coyote world. The rolling hills and flatlands spreading out from the Rockies almost always have some wind blowing. You just avoid the worst of it and learn to work with it most of the time.

If it is windy, I like to observe the wildlife or the domestic livestock in the distance to see if they're hearing my calls. If they pick up their heads, or turn their heads, it's an indicator that you're reaching out that far.

When it's too windy, you learn very quickly the futility of the situation.

One time, we were working a mile-long draw with the wind blowing down it pretty hard. We started at the bottom and had set up at several calling locations, working our way toward the head of the draw, where we felt there were some coyotes.

After several stands, we spotted two coyotes that came up out of our draw and went up a side draw. So we called to them. But no matter how hard we blew the call, they simply couldn't hear it. We figured the coyotes were pretty much done hunting and were heading for an area to be out of the wind for the rest of the day. They kept moving. They never heard us. And this despite the fact that they were always within view of us and were almost within shootable range.

You've got to learn how to call into the wind. You've also got to learn when to say no—the wind is too strong.

Working The Angles

Stands are normally set up so that you're not calling the same area that you called before. One of the nice things about following a ridgeline is that you can work one side, then move a distance, and go work the other side.

If you've got a creek drainage on both sides, you can work both creek bottoms that way. The wind will decide how close or far apart those stands might be.

Most of the time, it's important not to overlap your calling areas.

One tactic we like to use is to work points. Points might be protruding ridges, which might stick out into a basin, a creek, a draw, or a coulee. In the timber, it might be a protruding ridge that sticks out into the opening. Points are natural funneling areas to travel routes. They'll give you the uphill advantage and great visibility—at least a 180-degree sight picture. They also give you good concealment in your approach to a setup. In short, good stands are usually on points. When we go to an area, we always look for points.

Sometimes, a right-angle fence corner can do the same thing for you that a point does. All you have to do is sit at a fence corner and lean back against the post. That gives you the wide field of view. The fence provides the funnel to bring coyotes your way. If you're in sheep country, ranchers often use hog wire or sheep-tight fences and coyotes won't go through them, also funneling the coyotes toward you.

There have been some times, however, when I knew a coyote was in a particular area but either couldn't get him to respond or couldn't bring him all the way in. At times like those, I have maneuvered around and successfully called the coyote from a different angle.

One time we were down in the area near the Teddy Roosevelt National Grasslands in North Dakota and we were howling and a coyote was barking back at us. Barking like that is a sign that he's aware you're there. He'll just sit there and bark and bark.

One tactic we'll use in this situation is for the caller to continue howling, to keep the coyote occupied, and have a hunter slip down and try to work into a position to get a shot. In this case, that hunter never could get an angle on the coyote to shoot him.

So instead we went all the way around the drainage and worked that coyote from a different angle. We slipped over the hill quietly to get in position. We used a different howl, made it just three times, and pretty soon the coyote came in to investigate the new howl in the neighborhood. We got him at about one hundred yards.

Signals

Coyotes have keen eyesight. Coyotes also have a keen sense of hearing.

In other chapters, we've talked about how important it is for hunters to remain as motionless as possible. We've intimated that the sound of a human voice is like an alarm bell to coyotes and that you shouldn't talk much when you're out in coyote country.

For these reasons it's very critical for the hunter and caller

A squeaker call, like the Yote Squeaker, can be used to work coyotes that are coming in, to get them to come a little closer, or simply to signal your partner.

to be within sight of each other and to set up a formal or informal system of signals between them.

One of the things that has really worked well for us is using a squeaker as a signal. When somebody spots a coyote, they hit the squeaker. By looking in the direction where that person is looking, we all know where the coyote is. What helps us further is when the spotter slowly moves his rifle, pointing it in the direction where the coyote is coming in. That gives us the opportunity to spot the coyote as well.

There are other advantages to using squeaker signals instead of, let's say, hand signals. If you use a hand signal and your signal to get up and move is to raise a hand, your partner might be observing a coyote and your movement might alert the coyote that you're there.

Instead, we like to use four squeaks to signal that it's time to move. There's little movement involved. Then, the last thing we do before we move on is to mark down on the map where we've called, what we've killed, and what type of calls we used.

Sometimes you call in a female and know that perhaps the male is still in the area. We always feel it is beneficial to use a different type of calling sequence when we come back. By recording that in our notebook, we also have insights for the next time we come back. We have a better idea of what to try the next time.

Time and Calling

Probably the question that is asked most often of veteran coyote callers is how long do you stay in a stand and how long do you call.

For me, I like to stay at a stand fifteen to twenty minutes. You determine the length of time by how good the country is that you're looking over. It can also be determined by the time of year.

In winter, coyotes tend to come in more quickly. If there's one out there and he's interested, you should have him coming toward you within five to ten minutes. At a trot, it only

Winter is perhaps the best time to hunt coyotes. The animals are more active. Also, you've got the benefit of snow to help you spot tracks and the animals themselves. Jim Hamilton photo.

takes a coyote seven to eight minutes to cover a mile. If the coyote's running, he can make it in far less time than that.

In the summer and early fall, when the food supply is better, coyotes might not be that hungry. It might take up to twenty minutes or even a half-hour or more.

So overall, if you've got a good observation point and you've got good binoculars, you should have something spotted within the first twenty minutes or so.

Surprisingly, a person thinks a long time has passed. I like to use a watch. That way I know when I sat down, when I started calling, and when twenty minutes have passed. Sometimes you're sitting there and nothing is taking place and you think you've been there forever. And, actually, just ten minutes have passed.

In winter, after about twenty minutes, you generally feel pretty comfortable that you've given an area a decent chance and it's time to move on.

You don't have to be exact in your times. You don't have to—and really shouldn't—do it the same every time. But a watch certainly helps give you a general idea of what you're doing and how long you've been working a spot.

Aside from your concerns about how long you stay in a spot, another thing you should pay attention to in terms of time management is to vary your calling sequences within that time. Every caller falls into some kind of pattern that sounds good to him or her.

For me, I like to call for a couple of minutes to start with, then wait three to five minutes, then call for another minute, then wait three to four minutes. But I make a conscious effort to vary the sounds and vary the timing a bit.

If not, and if you call the same area often enough, a coyote living there can become aware of your calling habits. If you go back into that area and try the same routine over and over, you'll never call in a coyote that has heard you before.

If you vary your patterns, you can go back to the same area and call in different coyotes, or even call in the same coyote at a different time.

Howling

A lot of times I'll use the howl as a simple locator. But other times, I'll use the howl to let a coyote know that there is another coyote in the area.

That can work in several ways. Your howl might be interpreted as a simple assurance that a second coyote is in the area. It might also be interpreted as the howl of a coyote that has caught the rabbit or fawn that's making distress sounds. In that case, it can mean an easy meal.

Both ways, the howl makes a coyote more comfortable, feeling as though it's safe to come in. But you have to use it carefully. If you howl at every stand, you establish a pattern. At that point, you're establishing your own coyote territory. Another coyote might not come into that territory. It might be a young coyote that's not dominant enough to come in.

A loud howl in an area where sound doesn't travel very far can also be used to catch the attention of coyotes that might not be able to hear your other calls.

In one instance I can remember, a partner and I saw three coyotes that were in a lower field and then ran up into a timbered draw. We got our vehicle parked and then hurried over to a stack of hay bales—the only cover in the area—and started using a rabbit call, but nothing happened.

I told my partner that I wasn't sure that they were hearing us. I said, "Let me howl and see if I can get their attention." I howled, and that's exactly what happened. Immediately, one coyote came up out of the draw to the top of a hill and looked in our direction. Then I went to a rabbit call. He heard, and they all came in.

In the summer, the howl will sometimes work even better than in the winter. Coyotes are very territorial in the summer, especially if they've got a den nearby. Coyotes will come in to defend their territory. Sometimes, in fact, at that time of year, the howl is all you'll need. It'll usually bring in the male coyote first, then it will bring in the female. But sometimes, it's the other way around.

Distress Sounds

To me, distress sounds are very simple. People will talk about jackrabbits in distress, cottontails in distress, deer in distress. I don't think a coyote has a notebook that he packs around to which he can refer and then say, "Oh, that's a jackrabbit in distress."

From my observations, every critter makes distress sounds a little differently, even within the same species. The bottom line on all of them is that it sounds like some kind of animal in distress.

I really don't think you can blow a bad distress sound. It just has to sound like something in distress. It's high-pitched, but hits all frequencies high and low. It's a whine. It's a cry. It's something that's truly miserable and in pain. That's the common denominator. And that's what interests the coyote.

Let me illustrate. A friend of mine was driving to visit some friends in a river-bottom area. It was the spring of the year, the snow was melting, and it was muddy. They were coming around a corner in their vehicle and had to take a run at a hill.

As they came around the corner—this was in the time before infant car seats—a young child in the back seat fell over and bumped its head. It started crying. They stopped the car, got out, and came around to the back. The baby was still crying.

When they looked up, a coyote had come in within fifty yards of the car. The baby in distress had called him in.

Any call that evokes an animal that's in a hurting situation qualifies as a distress sound to a coyote. Everybody does a distress call a little differently. But each call suggests something in distress.

Stopping A Coyote

A lot of times a coyote will come in and never stop and give you a shot. He just comes in at a run or trot to look you over. He never stops moving. He never provides the sure shot. He just passes through and then is gone.

My preference for stopping a moving coyote for a shot is to use a squeaker call. It's a natural sound that won't educate an animal to be call-shy if the situation doesn't result in a killing shot. Jim Hamilton photo.

Some people have commented that all you need to do is holler at the coyote. The problem with that is that it instantly identifies you as a person. If you don't shoot the coyote, you're going to have a much tougher time ever getting that coyote to come in to you again.

One thing we have used successfully as a coyote stopper is a squeaker. The coyote hears the squeak. He stops. You have your shot. If one squeak doesn't work, try squeaking again. Sometimes the second squeak gets him.

Perhaps the best thing about using a squeaker as a stopper, however, is that if something does go wrong and you don't get your shot, or you don't deliver on the shot you take, it doesn't give you away as a person.

Second Shot

After I've called in and shot a coyote, or even if I called in and missed a coyote, I like to go right back to the call.

Most often, in situations like this, I'll use a canine-in-distress sound. If I've missed, sometimes that sound will turn the coyote around and give me a second chance at him. If I've hit a coyote, sometimes it will bring in a second coyote that might be its partner or simply another coyote in the area.

Using a canine-in-distress sound is not a sure thing. It won't work every time.

In the coyote-missed scenario, it's better to deliver a good shot the first time you pull the trigger. In the coyote-hit scenario, a smart second coyote will clear out of the country, no matter how good a caller you might be.

At times, I've also called in second coyotes using the rabbit-in-distress sound. Sometimes it takes a little while. Sometimes it happens right away.

The bottom line is that the opportunity to shoot a second coyote happens often enough that you ought to give it a try.

A friend of mine walked into an area with a partner once, and they were getting ready to set up to call. It never should have happened, but the partner's gun discharged. That

Hunters have tried a variety of decoys for coyotes and even worn coyote-head caps, but if you hunt an area with other gunners, you might be setting yourself up for an unwanted surprise if they mistake your cap for the real thing.

Chapter Five ■

made my friend understandably nervous, for safety reasons.

But they still were in an ideal spot, and rather than leave, they let things settle down for a while and started calling. Within a normal length of time, they called in a coyote and got him.

Second Coyote, Second Sounds

A lot of times when you're calling, you will call in a pair of coyotes. If you're looking to take them both, take note of how they come in.

You often find that one coyote is a little more dominant than the other coyote. The second coyote hangs back. When that happens, if you have both coyotes within range, shoot the farther coyote first. Then try to take the close one.

If you don't get the second coyote and you feel that this is its territory, you can go back into the same area either later that day or the following day and just use a howl.

Another tactic is to wait a week, or two weeks, then go back with your rabbit call. That's where a good notebook comes in. You can check what you used last time and try something different, perhaps a different type of distress call or perhaps a squeaker.

Knowing how to use different calls can help in other ways, too. In areas where there are a lot of people calling, that's also the time to go to something a little different— maybe the squeaker. Everybody else generally uses the rabbit call. The coyotes know that sound. Perhaps the squeaker is something new. Perhaps it's a bit different call.

When I came out with my Cow Talk elk call in the late 1980s, I got a call from a guy in Salt Lake City who said he hoped that I wasn't offended and didn't spread the word on it, but he had been using my cow call on coyotes and had called in twenty-seven coyotes in a month with it and taken every one.

He was using the high-pitched elk sounds as a distress call and having some great luck with a sound that coyotes in his area hadn't heard before.

Using a deer call and making deer-distress sounds with it can have the same results. It'll bring in deer. It will also bring in coyotes.

About fifteen years ago, I had a friend who was interested in calling in coyotes. We were using deer-distress sounds, and by midday, the coyote action had tailed off but we were still calling in deer with it.

Finally, the friend asked if he could give it a try. We sat there back to back, some distance apart. He started calling. I saw a couple of deer moving in the direction I was looking. Then I started to hear a pop, pop, pop sound behind me.

When I turned around, my friend was up on his feet, backing up. In front of him was an angry doe mule deer, up on its hind legs, striking at him with its front feet. That's something that can happen with those deer-distress sounds, too.

A Bit about Calls

The call we probably use the most is the Yote Buster call. It's an open-reed call. It uses a little lighter reed structure. It has a sliding cylinder. It's a good call for all kinds of sounds, including a coyote howl, bird sounds, prairie dog chirp, cottontail in distress, jackrabbit in distress, and the canine in distress.

Some guys I've seen will have many lanyards with calls around their necks. This one has a wrist lanyard. That way I can just have my binoculars around my neck.

We like to use open-reed calls in the West because it gets cold out here. You can take them apart and wipe the moisture out and be using them again in a few minutes. With closed-reed calls, you have to take them indoors and let them warm up and dry out.

There is no such thing as a sure-fire method in what's a sure-fire call. You use your best knowledge as to what will work at a given point in time.

For example, if you're around a prairie dog town, why not use a prairie dog chirp? It's a very effective call when there are prairie dogs around. Other times you want to make the rabbit sounds. An open-reed call allows you to make them all.

What call you eventually use, the one that's your call, is—

just that—up to you. Almost every hand-held coyote call on the market will work at some point in time. Mechanical calls have precise sounds, and they work, too.

If we have a preference for hand calls and open-reed calls, it's because we can tailor our sounds better. They're easier to pack around. They're easier to fix when weather conditions turn tough and we're several miles from our vehicle.

Dogging Coyotes

I first heard about dogging coyotes from a government trapper who said they used dogs during the summertime for predator control. He said it worked well.

The trapper said he'd have to tape my fingers together. He knew I'd want to shoot the coyote as soon as it got within range. And that's what happened. The dog brought the first coyote to within twenty-five yards, and it was going down-wind. The trapper made me wait. Eventually, we had a second coyote come in and then a third. We shot all three.

The basis for this is that coyotes do not like a dog in their territories in the summertime.

There have been instances of dogs getting killed by coyotes. Coyotes have killed ranch dogs that they've lured away. They've killed coyote dogs, too, that haven't been able to get back to the safety at the hunter's side.

When we came out with the videos *Dogging Coyotes* and *Dogging Coyotes II*, they created quite a stir in the coyote-hunting world.

Coyotes have been successfully called in by hunters for many, many years all through coyote country. But using a dog to bring coyotes within gun range was something of a new frontier to many coyote hunters. Until they saw the videos on it, some had never seen it done before.

The basic principle involved is that coyotes seem to be both attracted to, and aggressive toward, dogs. It's almost like a kid and candy. Coyotes just can't seem to stay away from a dog during the warm months of the year.

Coyotes in winter usually aren't as aggressive with dogs as they are during the summer, but there are times when a dog can still help you get a double.

Chapter Five ∎

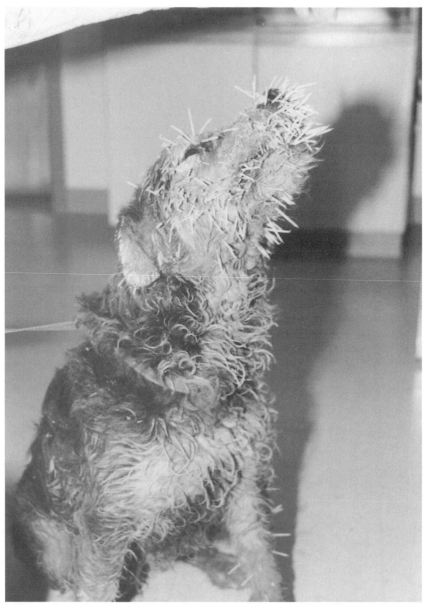

If you take a dog along with you, be sure to pack a pair of needle-nose pliers in case your dog runs into a porcupine along the way.

When you show up in their territory during the warm months, they'll aggressively try to chase the dogs out of the area. The coyotes will chase the dogs. The dogs will then chase the coyotes, if the coyotes lose interest.

In the process of give and take, the coyotes will become totally involved with the dogs and the dogs will gradually work the coyotes back toward you. The coyotes will bark, and howl, and often bring in other coyotes with them.

Our choice for coyote dogs is a breed called the Mountain Cur, though other breeds will work as coyote dogs as well. The key is to have them be big and strong enough to stand their ground, but not so aggressive that they'll simply chase the coyotes off and not come back to you. Like all good hunting dogs, these dogs have to be trained, and it's easier to train a new one if it has a trained dog to work with when it's young.

Dogging coyotes is done in conjunction with howling, distress calling, and squeaks. Those things bring the coyotes in so they can see the dogs. You still have to do all the homework of scouting and making a good setup. You can't move

Using a coyote dog can help you reduce coyote numbers quickly in areas where coyotes are numerous and a big problem for ranchers.

around unnecessarily, and you have to put your other hunting skills to work. But the key to it all is to have a good coyote dog for the coyotes to see once they come in. The end results are simply amazing, especially in being able to take multiple coyotes out of the same spot on a single setup.

I've sat on a stand and gotten as many as six coyotes to come in at a single time. When you've got multiple coyotes coming in, it's best to take the less aggressive coyotes first. The dog can then go back out and bring the more aggressive coyotes back.

Just keep taking the least aggressive coyote among the coyotes that are left and take the most aggressive coyote last. That way, it's an opportunity to remove a lot of coyotes from an area that's particularly thick with them and where they're causing the most problems.

Weather Fronts, Moon Phases

Let's face it, most of us go hunting when we have the opportunity to go hunting. We can't always go when the weather is perfect. We can't always wait for the right phase of the moon. When we have time to hunt coyotes, we go.

That doesn't mean, of course, that weather and moon phases don't play a role in success.

I believe that during times of the full moon, coyotes are more active at night and, as a result, are less active during the day. They're doing a lot of their hunting at night, and I think the full moon improves their success. This is almost always true in open-ground situations. It may not be so true during the winter when crusted snow may complicate their hunting and when there is less food available.

As to the weather, I can't help but believe that coyotes are much like other game animals. They become more active just ahead of weather fronts. They tend to lay low and weather the storm. If the storm is even a moderately long one, they grow hungry and will be out and active after a storm passes.

There really isn't much scientific data on this. It's just a feeling I've had after observing them.

Like many wildlife species, coyotes aren't very active during storms, but will be more active just ahead of a storm and after it passes. Jim Hamilton photo.

I do know that hot weather tends to make them less active than during times of cold weather. During times of hot weather, coyotes will be active early in the morning and again at evening. In cold weather, morning and evening are best, but you can pretty much work them all day long.

The bottom line for me has always been that if I have a chance to go out and call coyotes, I go—no matter what the phase of the moon—just as long as the weather is tolerable and the winds don't blow too hard.

Coyote Hot Spots

Some coyote spots are consistent producers. Maybe it's because these spots always have a good prey base. Maybe it's just the lay of the land, which funnels coyotes into them even after other coyotes are shot and removed.

If you find one of these areas, consider it to be golden. You can go back to these spots time after time, year after year, and take coyotes out of them.

The size of these spots can vary quite a bit. So does the way you hunt them.

In the boom-and-bust cycles of wildlife in the West, rabbits can be incredibly abundant in some years and provide plenty of food for hungry coyotes.

Sometimes, these spots are large and can be hunted in a conventional manner. But other hot spots might be small, real tight areas where coyotes hole up for the day. Perhaps it's just a small ravine in the middle of farmland or a big open flat. Maybe it's a patch of timber or brush. Maybe it's a piece of winter pasture in the middle of a more open area.

In places like these, you may get just one setup. You may also have to hunt them differently than you would a bigger area.

If the spot is small enough, perhaps all it takes is sneaking into the area and using a squeaker, or perhaps a soft rabbit sound. Howling or calling at full volume might be too much.

At times, you can figure out what the major attraction for coyotes is in these spots. Other times you can't. In either case, it's well worth your while to learn how to hunt spots like these and to recognize them when you come across them. They are coyote hot spots—the best kind of coyote spot you can have.

Coyotes That Hang Up

When a coyote comes in a ways, stops, then sits there and barks at you, it often means that he sees something that he doesn't like. Maybe it's a vehicle in the area. Maybe it's a reflection off your rifle scope or your binoculars. Maybe he has been called before and he's gotten nervous and he's not going to come any farther.

Once he sits out there and yap-yap-yaps at you, the game is up—at least for now. I usually try to sneak back out of the area. Or I wait until he gets tired and leaves. Then I sneak out.

Even if he's just four hundred yards out, what I don't believe in is to send a volley of bullets toward his area in hopes of hitting him.

I'd rather leave him alone and try something else another time, or use the buddy technique and have my partner sneak out and try to get in on him for a shot. I'll stay there and call and keep him barking. Then my partner can know his location as he works in toward him.

I've gone back into areas where coyotes have done that repeatedly—sometimes for a year or two years—and the coyote there always does the same thing. Once they start yapping or barking at you, what they're doing is telling everything in that area not to come in, something is wrong, and to leave you alone.

Night Calling

We've done night calling from time to time. There are some unique problems associated with it.

One of the first times I tried it, I had an aircraft landing light and the only way it would operate was off of a car battery. I put the car battery in a backpack and we walked out into the middle of a big open flat. My partner started doing the calling. We were sitting back to back.

As a result of all the calling, we called in about twenty deer all around us. We knew there were deer out there. There was a full moon, and we could see that well. We just didn't know if there was anything else out there.

My first observation of a coyote was when he was standing right at my foot. He sniffed the foot, then ran past me. I jabbed my partner in his back with my elbow and hit the lights. When the lights came on, all we could see were deer. We never did get him. We never even saw him again.

A lot of these things can and do happen when you hunt coyotes at night.

I should point out that in Wyoming, night calling is legal with written landowner permission. It's not legal everywhere to use an artificial light. It's not legal to hunt at night everywhere. Check your local regulations or call a game warden if you have any doubts about your own area.

Often what we'll do when calling at night is to drive a vehicle into a high-visibility area like a hay pasture or a creek bottom. We'll sit right in the vehicle and call from there. It's a little more comfortable than sitting in a snowdrift or having to carry a battery pack. Then I'll use a cassette tape player and an external speaker. It's a lot easier.

Many of the other rules apply. Call into the wind. Expect the coyote to head to the downwind side. Other rules are new. Try not to do it on a full-moon night. They can see the vehicle too easily and won't come in as close.

To be truthful, I've done it the other way, too. I've sat on

Coyotes tend to get very active toward evening and will hunt throughout the night. But night hunting provides its own special problems. Jim Hamilton photo.

a haystack at night. I've used the battery pack light. But maybe I'm getting too old to do these nighttime maneuvers the way I used to. That warm vehicle seems more and more appealing as the years go by.

And, of course, I can always get those coyotes during the daytime when I want to. That leaves the nighttime for snoozing under warm blankets—all in all, a very good place to be on a cold winter's night.

CHAPTER SIX

ODDS AND ENDS

Here are the top five things that you should have learned from this book so far—and they're ranked in order of importance:

1. You have to find and be in an area that has an ample coyote population. It doesn't do you any good to call in an area that doesn't have many coyotes.

2. Make a proper setup in your area, and make a proper approach to your stand. While at the stand, remain still when you're there and don't make any radical movements. That's the best camo pattern you can have. Make no foreign noises.

3. Call with favorable weather conditions, with wind being the primary factor, when you make your stand and when you make your calls.

4. Do your calling at the best times of the day. That's within the first three hours after sunrise or the last two hours before dark.

5. Produce the proper sounds with your call. Learn all the sounds—the howls, the distress sounds, the squeaker. Then keep your volume under control—use only as much volume as you need.

To become a true coyote hunter, you need to start calling in coyotes. The more you work at it, the more success you'll find and the more you'll learn. The more success you find and the more you learn, the better your chances at becoming a truly great coyote hunter.

The Old War On Coyotes

If you look back over the past hundred years or so, there haven't been too many things that haven't been tried to wage war against the coyote. At some point in time, I even think that some folks had the notion that they were winning the war. At other times, they figured the war was totally lost. In truth, I think we're somewhere in between.

Traps and snares can be effective tools to remove problem coyotes, but many trappers don't go after coyotes anymore because the pelts aren't worth as much as they used to be.

Coyotes have been poisoned, trapped, run over, drowned, hunted on land, hunted from the air. Each method has taken some coyotes. Each claims its successes. But coyotes haven't just persisted. They've thrived. It's a testament to the durability and adaptability of this predator.

An uncle of mine in the Dakotas talks about young people in his area who run and gun coyotes on the weekend. A guy at the wheel of a vehicle would chase any coyote he saw cross-country. Either a guy in the back or a guy leaning out of the window would shoot when the coyote was in range.

They'd run and gun like that on the weekend, then repair their vehicles almost every night for the rest of the week to do it again. In one year, they got two hundred coyotes doing that. They became pretty good mechanics, too, with all the repairs they had to make.

Aerial hunting is a method of choice among some governmental agencies and contract pilots, especially in areas where coyotes are preying heavily on sheep and livestock.

In past years, I used to run coyotes with greyhounds. We had a pickup truck equipped with a box in the back that had a pull rope so we could lower the gate and let the hounds jump out.

If we jumped a coyote, the chase was on. We'd drive the truck as close to the coyote as we could, then pull the rope. Sometimes, we would run several bunches of hounds together. Everybody had his own pack.

People pursue coyotes on snowmobiles in winter to get within shotgun range. At times this, too, can be effective. A friend once got fourteen coyotes in two hours one morning. The rancher was very happy. He had been having some real problems with a dense coyote population.

But another time, we traveled a hundred miles on a snowmobile after just one coyote—off and on for an entire day—following the animal and then his tracks when we lost sight of him. After all that, we never got him. He went down a badger hole.

Trapping used to be a popular method to take coyotes. There was a time when coyote pelts went for $100 to $150 apiece for top animals. Everybody went after coyotes—

trapping and hunting. They killed a lot.

But since then, the fur market has gone down to the point that now there are very few people trapping. There are a few hard-core trappers out that are making a little money at it. But most trappers have given it up.

Poisoning of coyotes was done into the early 1970s, and it, too, killed coyotes. It killed some non-target animals, too, especially if one wasn't real careful about how one did it. That's among the reasons why it's not being done anymore.

Other coyote control measures were used as well. Many of them either aren't used at all or aren't very popular anymore. But the bottom line is that none of them wiped out the coyote. In the end, the coyote won the war.

Coyotes Today

There's a bumper sticker in the rural West. It reads: "Eat American Lamb—10 million coyotes can't be wrong."

There's a joke, too. It states that an old couple decided to will the family sheep ranch to their kids. The kids refused to take it and said they'd sue the old couple for child abuse if they ever tried to give it to them again.

The old war on coyotes may be over—at least as far as much of the fighting goes—but coyotes live on. They have a real impact on ranch operations, and ranchers fight them by putting llamas with their herds, buying special breeds of dogs, hiring sheepherders when they can find them, and putting pressure on governmental agencies to give them some coyote control.

Wildlife agencies throughout many states are also finding that coyotes can have a big impact on deer, antelope, and other species. When rabbit and mouse populations go through declines, coyotes change their hunting methods. They go after big game, even adult big game. Always, coyotes are on the lookout for fawns.

In times of low deer or antelope populations, coyotes can have an especially significant impact. They'll hold big-game populations down. They can plunge population declines

Coyotes can be effective predators on big game like deer and antelope, too, hunting alone for fawns or gathering in packs to hunt adults in winter when other food sources aren't available. Jim Hamilton photo.

Chapter Six ■

even deeper. In some places, they're the biggest factor controlling game numbers aside from devastatingly tough winters or lost habitat.

What is being done about the times when, and places where, coyote populations boom?

Studies have shown that coyote-control measures like aerial hunting can have an impact on big-game survival. But it certainly isn't cheap. In one Montana study, for example, it cost a state agency $104 for every coyote shot in the study area from a Super Cub airplane. The helicopter gunning cost $294 per coyote.

Some rural communities have gone back to the old bounty system to try to increase the number of coyotes taken in their area. Other communities or groups hold coyote-calling derbies where prize money is awarded to individuals or two-hunter teams who take the greatest number of coyotes in a day, a weekend, or a longer period of time.

Still other communities in the West are starting to promote coyote hunting as a tourist attraction, hoping to spur an influx of coyote hunters from far away to come visit their town and help trim back coyote numbers.

And some counties have hired their own trappers to try to get a handle on coyote numbers, by trapping, hunting, aerial gunning, almost whatever it takes—legally—to provide some relief.

Perhaps it's not the war against coyotes it once was, but it's an ongoing battle in many rural areas. Who's winning? Many would say the coyotes are doing very, very well.

The Coyote Hunter

Welcome to the future of coyote management. That future is the coyote hunter.

Think about it. Where else are you going to turn? Poisons are out. Trapping isn't profitable. Aerial gunning is real expensive. Specialized trucks and hounds are only somewhat less expensive. And not everyone can be his or her own mechanic with the vehicles that are damaged by the chase-and-gun technique.

Hunters are destined to become the management tool of the future for coyote populations. Other options simply won't be available anymore.
Jim Hamilton photo.

Chapter Six

The best option for today and into the future is the coyote hunter, the person who can go into an area with a dense coyote population and use his skills with a call and a good rifle to reduce coyote numbers.

Coyote hunters are never going to wipe out entire coyote populations. And, in truth, they shouldn't. If you want to talk philosophy, coyotes have always been a part of the West and are a growing part of other portions of North America as well. They're a truly impressive predator, trying to scratch out a living from some of the harshest environments on the continent, too.

But just because they deserve a place in the whole scheme of things, that doesn't mean they don't need a little managing. Individual problem coyotes for ranchers need to be removed. Coyote populations that grow out of control need to be cut back to lessen the impact on our deer and antelope herds and other wildlife species.

Controlling coyote populations is an ongoing problem. It always will be, simply because of the nature of coyotes themselves. Calling coyotes will teach you that.

No matter what you do, if you do it long enough, the coyotes will adapt to it after a certain length of time. You have to change tactics. You have to be knowledgeable. You have to be effective.

It's my contention that by encouraging the hunting of more coyotes, we can help improve fawn survival among wildlife species. We can make a difference in ranch areas that are being overrun by coyotes. We can at least make a strong effort at using hunters to manage coyote populations.

For hunters who want to learn to do just that, here's the book on it. All we ask is that you honor landowners' rights and always ask permission before you hunt on someone's place. Make sure, as well, that you have the proper licenses—some states require them. And, finally, understand that you're not going to become an expert coyote hunter overnight.

There will always be coyotes. Hunting coyotes is not going to eliminate the coyote in its entirety. It never will. But coyote hunting can help to manage coyote populations and keep them in balance with the world around them, so that all wildlife—and all people—can coexist with them in coyote country.

ABOUT THE AUTHORS

Don Laubach is the founder and president of E.L.K., Inc. He is the inventor and patent holder of several game calls, including the "Cow Talk" call, the first cow elk call available to the public. More recently, he developed the universal coyote call, the "Yote Buster," and the "Yote Squeaker." With co-author Mark Henckel, his books include *Elk Talk, The Elk Hunter, Deer Talk,* and *Elk Tactics.* Laubach also was involved in creating a number of successful videos with legendary filmmaker Gordon Eastman and has more recently begun creating videos on his own on coyotes, elk, deer, and other game animals. All are available from E.L.K., Inc., P.O. Box 85, Gardiner, MT, 59030.

Merv Griswold has spent the past forty years chasing coyotes in South Dakota and Wyoming. A South Dakota native, he began calling and hunting coyotes, trapping coyotes, and running greyhounds. After moving to Wyoming, he did extensive coyote-control work on a county-funded bounty program that involved calling, denning, trapping, and gunning for an aerial hunter. More recently, he has used dogs for decoying coyotes. With Don Laubach, he has worked on the videos *Dogging Coyotes, Bustin' Coyotes,* and *Dogging Coyotes II.* Griswold lives in Gillette, Wyoming, owns High Plains Outfitters, and raises Mountain Curs for coyote dogs.

Mark Henckel is the outdoor editor of the *Billings* (Montana) *Gazette.* In addition to writing *Elk Talk, The Elk Hunter, Deer Talk,* and *Elk Tactics* with Don Laubach, Henckel also wrote *A Hunter's Guide to Montana* and has authored six children's books on the outdoors as well. He has won national awards for his newspaper and magazine writing from the Outdoor Writer's Association of America and has received a number of other honors from outdoor organizations. Henckel lives in Park City, Montana.

Other books available from E.L.K., Inc., P.O. Box 85, Gardiner, MT 59030

Elk Talk

Your Guide to Finding Elk, Calling Elk, and Hunting Elk with a Rifle, Bow and Arrow, or Camera

The Elk Hunter

The Ultimate Source Book on Elk and Elk Hunting from Past to Present, for the Beginning and Expert Alike

Deer Talk

Your Guide to Finding, Calling, and Hunting Mule Deer and Whitetails, with Rifle, Bow, or Camera

Elk Tactics

Advanced Strategy for Hunting and Calling Elk

For product information, orders, or free catalog, call toll-free E.L.K., Inc., 1-800-272-4355. Visa and MasterCard accepted. Web site: www.elkinc.com. E-mail: elkinc@mcn.net